Jacob Weidenmann
pioneer landscape architect

Jacob Weidenmann
(1829–1893),
landscape architect

Jacob Weidenmann

pioneer landscape architect

Rudy J. Favretti

Fellow, American Society of Landscape Architects

Cedar Hill Cemetery Foundation, Incorporated
in cooperation with Wesleyan University Press

5 4 3 2 1

ISBN 978-0-8195-6847-2 (0-8195-6847-3)

Published by Cedar Hill Cemetery Foundation Inc.
453 Fairfield Avenue
Hartford CT 06114

Distributed by Wesleyan University Press
Middletown CT 06459
In association with
University Press of New England
Lebanon NH 03766

Designed by Nathan Garland LLC
New Haven CT 06510

Printed by Amilcare Pizzi s.p.a.
20092 Cinisello Balsamo (Milano) Italy

Library of Congress Cataloging-in-Publication Data
Favretti, Rudy J.
Jacob Weidenmann: pioneer landscape architect / Rudy J Favretti. — 1st ed.
p. cm.
Includes bibliographical references and index.
ISBN 978-0-8195-6847-2 (cloth: alk. paper)
1. Weidenmann, Jacob, 1829-1893. 2. Landscape architects — United States —
Bibliography. I. Title.

SB470.W435F38 2007
712.092 — dc22   2007004778
[B]

Contents

Preface

As Chairman of the Board of Directors of Cedar Hill Cemetery and Cedar Hill Foundation, it is my distinct pleasure to acquaint readers with a fascinating new history of Jacob Weidenmann, one of America's pioneer landscape architects.

Weidenmann's life began in the old world, but his work affected his adopted America in tangible ways by bequeathing us a uniquely American form of interment—the "open lawn" cemetery. Cedar Hill, at the southern terminus of Fairfield Avenue in Hartford, Connecticut, remains one of the few examples of Weidenmann's art and precepts. We are proud to have carefully preserved Cedar Hill Cemetery following his design concepts, as well as, the principles that he laid down as its first superintendent from 1865–1870. Today Cedar Hill is listed on the National Register of Historic Places.

In his own way, Weidenmann enjoyed the approbation of his famous peer and colleague, Frederick Law Olmsted, and today he retains an enthusiastic twenty-first century champion in the scholar, educator and landscape architect, Rudy J. Favretti, this book's author.

Professor Favretti, a nationally-known and much respected authority, is not only a Connecticut native but also, most felicitously, has been a member of Cedar Hill's Board. His mentoring has helped the Cedar Hill family retain and expand Jacob Weidenmann's timeless concepts.

I write this preface in 2006, the 150th anniversary of Weidenmann's journey to America. His brilliant design for Cedar Hill has resulted in a landscape of repose and is the ultimate place of rest for noted local and national figures in politics, commerce, and the arts, as well as, their friends and neighbors who merely appreciated beauty. His grounds contain an extraordinary arboretum of specimen trees and other plants, and our monuments comprise a grand outdoor sculpture gallery. Diverse wildlife finds sanctuary in our unspoiled groves and meadows.

The publication of *Jacob Weidenmann, Pioneer Landscape Architect*, adds a new dimension to Cedar Hill's reputation as a repository of history, and it is our proud intention to continue this tradition of honoring those who rest in our lovely landscape.

Robert L. Newell, Jr.

Foreword

Marguerite Weidenmann wrote an account of her father as a little boy telling how he had been put to bed one hot summer night in the family home in Winterthur, Switzerland. The room was shuttered to keep the light and birds out and yet to allow any breeze to circulate. Young Jacob was abruptly awakened by a loud noise in the street below, and being the curious and active child that he was, he squirmed down from his bed, toddled across the floor, and pulled himself up onto the broad windowsill so that he could lean against the shutters and peer through to see what made the noise. Jacob's mother, hearing his footsteps, came into the room just as the shutters began to spring open. She was just in time to grab little Jacob by his nightshirt, saving him from falling to the pavement below. Thereafter, whenever she related this story, Mother Weidenmann said that Jacob was "born under a veil of good luck."

He was a lucky man. He came from a family of means and had every opportunity as a child. He had the benefit of a college education in times when few received one, with no pressure from his parents to pursue a field of their liking rather than his. His family was even willing to finance his extensive travels throughout Europe and America so that he might broaden his education through varied experiences. When he finally settled down, he had a successful career as one of the leading and best-trained landscape architects of his century.

Why, then, has there been so little written about Jacob Weidenmann? David Schuyler wrote a superior essay on him as the introduction to the reproduction of Weidenmann's book, *Beautifying Country Homes*, published by the American Life Foundation and Study Institute and the Athenaeum of Philadelphia in 1978. It is very well written and documented, and presents what was known about Weidenmann at that time. Without it, Jacob Weidenmann would be virtually unknown today. There are a few biographical pieces in encyclopedias and in textbooks, but aside from these nothing else exists.

There appear to be several reasons for the dearth of material on Weidenmann. Aside from a few written pieces and sketches, and the collection of plates for his *American Garden Architecture* that his daughter gave to the New York Public Library in 1934, his family destroyed his papers, journals, and plans after his death. Also, landscape plans are fragile and do not last, especially when rolled-up and stored in hot, dry attics, or moist basements, so researchers have not been able to find many.

One of the biggest problems in researching the career of Jacob Weidenmann is trying to sort out who did what during the nineteen years that he was associated with Frederick Law Olmsted, particularly the first nine of them when their collaboration was especially intense. Marguerite Weidenmann, in her twelve-page sketch of her father's career, attributes several projects to him. Yet in *The Master List of Design Projects of the Olmsted Firm, 1857–1950*, the same projects are attributed to Olmsted. The same thing occurs with Weidenmann's years in Chicago. His daughter claims several projects for her father, but the great architect William LeBaron Jenny, with whom Weidenmann collaborated, claims the same ones. It is at this point that several Weidenmann scholars have given up.

As this book will show, Weidenmann's "veil of good luck" evolved into a vast scrim totally obscuring his work. He was over-shadowed by the great landscape architects and architects with whom he associated, though they sought his assistance. Few scholars have been able to devote the time to see through this fuzzy scrim and sort it all out, a long and arduous task.

My wife and I set out to unravel the facts relating to Weidenmann's career over forty years ago, working toward this goal a little at a time. In my retirement, more time became available for intensive research. Hours were spent trying to reconstruct Weidenmann's life and career with what little material was available. We traveled to Switzerland to research his early life, checked the vital statistics regarding his family, reviewed the records of the technical institute where he went to college, and researched immigration records, and birth and death certificates in America. I then read the Olmsted Papers in the Library of Congress for the nineteen years of the Olmsted-Weidenmann alliance, in which I found much correspondence between the two, as well as bills and statements for various projects.

Where no information existed regarding certain projects, I searched the background of the clients; their obituaries often carried valuable leads. Newspaper articles, though not often complete, gave some information and ideas for further investigation. Archival collections in communities where he worked sometimes yielded good results. For example, at the Iowa State Historical Society Library, I found one of his original and uncatalogued plans for the Polk-Hubbell Residential Park tucked away inside an old atlas. All of these resources solved significant parts of the Weidenmann puzzle, though by no means is every aspect of his varied life and work resolved.

It will be noticed in the photograph of the Weidenmann tombstone, pictured at the end of this book, that his name is spelled ending with one "n." Throughout this book I have used the original spelling of his name as it appears in the Vital Records of the City of Winterthur, Switzerland, spelled "Weidenmann." After Jacob Weidenmann came to America, he sometimes dropped one "n," though most of the time he spelled his name as originally given, as he did on all of the books he wrote and most of his drawings. Apparently, using the single "n" was an attempt to Anglicize the name, a practice that his daughter Marguerite followed consistently.

Jacob Weidenmann is worthy of a full account of his career. During his lifetime, many commented on his talents. No less a luminary than Frederick Law Olmsted wrote to the City of Rochester, New York, in 1888, when they were planning Highland Park: "There are in this country to my knowledge but two other (properly speaking) landscape designers . . . who have the experience that would specially qualify them to advise you. One of them is H.W.S. Cleveland . . . ; the other is J. Weidenmann." In addition to being considered a top-notch landscape architect, Weidenmann was one of the first to promote the establishment of landscape architecture programs in universities in this country. The curriculum that he suggested parallels quite closely what is being taught in accredited landscape architecture schools today, minus the technological aspects that he could not foresee. His interest in education is also expressed in his writings, which are presented in a clear, organized style, amply illustrated with his own renderings. This book will show that Weidenmann was an exemplary landscape architect, one who helped raise the profession to its present stature.

Chapter One

Formative Years

A legend prevailed in the Weidenmann family about an ancient ancestor who came to a place somewhere within the boundaries of present-day Switzerland from the land of the Vikings in far off Norway. Little else is known about this ancient immigrant except that one of his descendents in the thirteenth century operated a ferry boat. One day, during a violent storm when the boat capsized, he valiantly saved the life of one of his distinguished passengers by swimming with him to shore. The victim was supposedly a Hapsburg Duke, who in appreciation, made this oarsman a free man, with all privileges appertaining, and he also awarded him a coat-of-arms with the central figure on the shield an oarsman, surrounded by a grove of willow trees; hence the name Weidenmann, or "willow man." This coat-of-arms was cherished by the family and handed down for many generations.

By the early nineteenth century, a descendent of this legendary ferryman named Jacob Weidenmann (1798–1864) was well established in Winterthur, Switzerland, as a government customs officer with responsibilities for testing and appraising all cotton imported into Switzerland, a highly respected and well-paying position. Weidenmann soon married Elise Gubbler (1799–1893), an attractive member of the upper social class of Winterthur, known for her beauty as well as her native intelligence, and who also had a reputation as a keen businesswoman.

The Weidenmanns became the parents of five children; the second son, the subject of this monograph, was named Jacob for his father. He was born on August 24, 1829, in the family's comfortable home at Strauss Marktgasse 70, Winterthur's busy business district. To this day the street has shops on the ground floors with residences on the upper stories. At intervals along the street there are fountains and statues, mostly at intersections, and many of the original magnificent buildings of the eighteenth and nineteenth centuries remain. Unfortunately, a post World War II structure has replaced the building where the Weidenmanns resided.

The younger Jacob Weidenmann was an intelligent, inquisitive, lively, and mischievous child, according to his family. He performed very well in school and expressed an early interest in design and architecture. Fortunately his parents encouraged these interests, and when the time came for him to specialize in his chosen field, they had the means to support his education. However, before he entered college, young Jacob Weidenmann worked for a short period for an architect friend of his parents, A. M. Forte, who had a home and office in Geneva. This experience provided an opportunity to test his interests and to be certain of his career choice.

In 1847, Jacob and his brother Heinrich, a law student, were residing in Munich, in Bavaria. Jacob was enrolled for four semesters at the Akademie der Bildenden Kunste in the general program. He then studied in the Fine Arts program for two additional semesters under the director of the Academie, the renowned muralist Wilhelm von Kaulbach (1805–1874). His murals popularized historic events such as the "Battle of the Huns," the "Crusaders," and the "Reformation." Others were melodramatic illustrations of the works of Goethe and Shakespeare. His vast paintings covered "acres of walls in Munich and Berlin."

To enlarge his technical training, Weidenmann then enrolled at University of Karlsruhe, under Professor Eisenlohr, where he studied architecture and engineering. It was this additional training that later enabled him to design and draw his own plans for drainage projects, road planning, and building construction.

Jacob Weidenmann did well in his studies, but he was not satisfied to limit them just to the classroom. On his own initiative, wanting to enlarge his knowledge of sketching and painting, he frequented the ateliers of well-known artists, such as that of Johann Rudolf Koller (1828–1905), a Swiss painter from Zurich. Koller, after studying in Düsseldorf and Paris, went to Munich and painted with a group of artists called the "Schweizer." He eventually returned to Zurich and specialized in painting pastoral and animal scenes.

Many of these established artists welcomed the young Weidenmann into their ateliers, and they often referred to him as "Buberl" (little boy). One wonders the extent to which his association with them, the painters of large murals and natural landscapes, affected his becoming an artist of the landscape who worked in a three dimensional medium. Certainly his skills in sketching and as a watercolorist were enhanced by these experiences.

While in Zurich in 1850, presumably studying with Koller, Weidenmann also enrolled in a course of study in botany at the Botanical Garden. He claimed even that if the course only gave him "superficial knowledge," it would stand him in good stead when he later decided to become a landscape architect.

The Weidenmann family's secure financial position enabled young Jacob to travel abroad after completing his studies. He went first to Paris, and then on to London. Eventually he sailed to the United States, having a miserable voyage due to illness caused by a severe gastric upset and fever, probably brought on by "unsanitary conditions as well as improper food" aboard ship. He became so ill that he feared death, and perhaps even wished it. Soon after arriving in New York, though, he regained his strength, and each day he extended his walks in the City. On certain afternoons he "walked with friends into the country [the area of present 34th street and north], then a stretch of bare lands with here and there a shanty or shack, with goats and now and then a cow, turned out to graze among the weeds."

It was his restless, inquisitive nature, combined with the lure of the gold rush that attracted Jacob to the California territory in order to go prospecting. There is no evidence that he struck it rich there, but he did have some success because there is a nugget of gold, filed in a tiny envelope, in the Special Collections of the New York Historical Society. The label indicates that it was panned by Jacob Weidenmann in "the mines of California, 1850–51."

Weidenmann subsequently heard of the possibility of going to Panama to work on the railroad that was being constructed across the Isthmus, forerunner of the Canal, by the Universal Inter-Oceanic Canal Company, headed by the builder of the Suez Canal, Ferdinand de Lesseps. Weidenmann signed on as an assistant engineer.

Soon after arriving, he saw his co-workers dying off like flies from malaria and other tropical diseases. The Company's carpenter shop was kept busy building pine coffins, and many of the construction crew spent full time digging graves. Jacob Weidenmann wanted out, but this was not easy to do because the Company controlled the limited transportation leaving the region. The Company kept strict surveillance over who was arriving or departing in an attempt to keep as many of their workers as possible.

Weidenmann and a friend hatched a scheme: they would rise before dawn and carefully leave the area on foot over one of the few unguarded roads.

> By the time the sun was up they had succeeded to put considerable distance between themselves and the camp.

After a while the day became oppressively hot, and they decided to rest a while. They had taken a small portion of bread…and this they ate while resting. [They] then resumed their march. When night came, they took turns watching and sleeping, and by sunrise were again on their way. It happened on the third day, when having noticed a tree of peculiar growth the previous morning that they saw the same [tree] before them again. They had walked around in a circle. It was then that all hope forsook them, and they gave themselves up to complete despair. Sinking down on a large stone, side by side, they began to talk of their home, which they believed they would never see again, they told of their father and mother, and all those dear to them, and as they talked tears came to their eyes, and soon they both cried like two little children.

Once the tears subsided they noticed a river nearby, the Chagres River, and further in the distance they spotted a boat propelled with large poles by two "Negro" slaves in their loin cloths, with the Indian owner as the only passenger. Weidenmann and his friend hailed the boat, and finally their shouts were heard. The Weidenmann account of this story does not record where this boatman took them, but it is presumed that they went on to Callao, Peru, by boat. It was a village of limited opportunity with a hotel with "most primitive accommodations," where the owner told him to take "his morning toilet on the beach." Soon Jacob moved on to Lima, slightly to the north.

Shortly thereafter Weidenmann found employment at the Hacienda, "LaMolina," located fifteen kilometers from Lima, as consulting architect and engineer. Apparently the owners were expanding their Hacienda for which Weidenmann drew plans and supervised construction. It is not known exactly how long he stayed in Lima, possibly two years, but long enough to make many friends, including the owners of "La Molina" with whom he lived, and to save enough money to perform an extraordinarily impulsive act of charity. One day in the slave market, he saw a poor slave family being sold, each member separately, and with his savings he purchased them all and then set them free.

We have no details of Weidenmann's work on "La Molina," but it seems that the Hacienda was new, and that he was hired to expand the estate into a large working farm with extensive landscaped grounds. This appears to have been his first commission as an architect/landscape architect. In the twentieth century, the Hacienda

Weidenmann's quick sketch of Hacienda "La Molina," Peru.
The sketch is signed: "1852, J. Weidenmann.
Nach der Natur gezeichnet." (Drawn from nature.)

expanded greatly to become "La Escuela Nacional de Agricultura" (the National Agriculture School), and today it is known as the highly regarded "Universidad Agraria" of Peru. The large campus, approached from three main avenues, has six major buildings that house the departments and laboratories of chemistry, botany, horticulture, genetics, zoology, animal husbandry, and agronomy, as well as the library and supportive services.

Letters from home begged Jacob to return. The family was in distress. Heinrich Weidenmann had completed his law studies in Munich and had begun the practice of law with great success. However, military service caught up with him, and while on duty he contracted a severe cold with complications. Antibiotics did not exist in those days, and he died at age twenty seven. The year was 1853.

Jacob Weidenmann remained in Europe for a few years but we don't know exactly what occupied his time. Some have speculated that he traveled about studying architecture and landscapes, while others have suggested that it was during this period that he became interested in the field of horticulture, an area in which he later excelled. By the late summer of 1856, his restless nature spurred him on to New York again, a place that he liked and where he intended to settle. He obviously was intrigued by the rapidly expanding city and wanted to be part of the action.

On board the ship "*Argonne*," he became acquainted with a young lady named Anna Margaretha Schwager, or Svacher (1838–1909), who was traveling with her mother to visit a younger brother in New York. Mrs. Schwager was the wife of a pensioned military officer. Her family now lived in France, though they were originally from Wurzburg, Germany. Jacob and Anna fell in love, and before the ship pulled into port, they became engaged to wed (another impulsive decision). Soon after landing, they were married on October 13, 1856. Mrs. Schwager, after a visit with her son, returned to France. Jacob and Anna made their home at 50 Frankfort Street, and he rented an office at 21 Suffolk Street where he began his practice of landscape gardening.

Pivotal Years

The four years following Jacob and Anna Weidenmann's wedding were significant in many ways. His restless urge to travel had been satisfied, and he was ready to settle down and launch a career. There is no doubt that during his travels throughout Europe, and North and South America, he was impressed by the natural landscapes that he saw. People whom he encountered, who were engaged in designing landscapes and growing the plants for them, influenced him. His interest began to focus on the field of landscape architecture then called landscape gardening. While an ancient art, there were few professionals in America practicing it who were as well trained as Weidenmann with a strong academic background in art, architecture, engineering, and horticulture, and with a clear understanding of the importance of working with nature to design effective landscapes. It remains a mystery as to how he knew to train himself in this way.

When Weidenmann arrived in New York in October 1856, the City was still a growing town. Most streets were still gravel, with hogs rooting on some of them, and as mentioned earlier, the area north of 34th Street was open country, much of it a wasteland. The city was abuzz about the future central park that the city fathers had finally decided to have designed and built. The competition for the park's design was to start in 1857. William Cullen Bryant (1794–1878), poet and editor of the *New York Evening Post,* had been badgering the City to create such a place, quoting from essays which had been written by the eminent horticulturist/landscape gardener, Andrew Jackson Downing, that said in essence that citizens in cities needed parks in which to relax and play; one had only to witness the use of rural cemeteries for that purpose. The rural cemetery movement had started in 1831 whereby attractive sites, complete with as many natural features as possible—trees, water, undulating ground—were turned into burial grounds. The problem was that these cemeteries were filling up with burials, and many considered their use as recreation spaces disrespectful to the dead.

As Weidenmann met people in New York who were related to his new field of interest, he no doubt found many still mourning the tragic death of Andrew Jackson Downing (1815-1852), who drowned in a steam boat accident on the Hudson River as he was attempting to save fellow passengers. Downing was a prolific writer, and his *Treatise on the Theory and Practice of Landscape Gardening* (1841), had had five printings before his death. It was the first book published in the United States completely devoted to the field of landscape gardening (Bernard McMahon's *American Gardener's Calendar,* published in 1806, contained some information on the subject, but the book was largely horticultural). For many years, well into the twentieth century, the *Treatise* was reprinted, and it remained the most complete and most used book on the subject.

In his *Treatise*, Downing acknowledged that he was adapting theories advanced by earlier practitioners in England, proponents of the English landscape style which involved using the natural landscape as the basis for landscape designs, and working with nature to create walks and plantings following the dictates of contours and natural conditions rather than following traditional, symmetrical plans. Downing acknowledged his debt to early designers, such as William Kent (1685–1748), Lancelot "Capability" Brown (1716–1783), and Humphry Repton (1725–1808), as well as to the proponents of the picturesque movement, Uvedale Price (1747–1829), Richard Payne Knight (1750–1824), and others.

Throughout this book the word *picturesque* will be used to describe certain landscape effects, so perhaps a digression is needed to define the word whose very meaning has changed over the years since first used in reference to landscapes in the late eighteenth century. It is not an easy word to define in the landscape sense; even two of the strongest proponents of the picturesque, the gentleman-neighbors in Herefordshire, Sir Uvedale Price and Richard Payne Knight, had a falling out over the definition.

Simply defined, the picturesque meant the creation of scenes within the landscape that would draw an artist to his canvas, paints, and easel, with an urgent desire to record them, or as we would say today, painterly scenes, like a picture. The early writers on the picturesque divided these scenes into two types, the beautiful and the sublime. The beautiful were equated to serenity and smoothness of objects in the landscape, while the sublime referred to ruggedness and lively motion. The paintings of Claude Lorraine with placid lakes, or gently flowing streams, bordered by easy paths along them, all surrounded by rounded hills and round-form trees, were considered ideal examples of the *beautiful*. On the other hand, those of Salvator Rosa, which portrayed peaked mountains, or craggy ledges, with waterfalls tumbling over them, and jaggedly-formed trees growing out of crevices in the ledges with a tangle of vines growing up them, were called *sublime*.

The picturesque movement was a reaction to the landscapes designed earlier by William Kent and Lancelot Brown, which Price and Knight and their followers considered "monotonous . . . uncommonly mean, contracted, and perverse." Together they referred to Brown's large, one-species tree groupings as "clumps," and Knight, in his lengthy poem entitled *The Landscape*, derided Repton's work as:

> Prim gravel walks, through which we winding go,
> In endless serpentines that nothing show.

The picturesque was a major topic of discussion among landscape gardeners resulting in more books and essays on the subject including a popular book by Edmund Burke entitled *A Philosophical Inquiry Into the Origins of Our Ideas of the Sublime and the Beautiful* (1825). As the century progressed, and by the time Downing published his *Treatise* in 1848, the definition of the picturesque had changed. He defined "the kind of beauty we may hope to produce in Landscape Gardening" as "the beautiful" and the "picturesque," beautiful still defined as above, but now picturesque is defined as equal to what had been called the sublime, or rugged scenes. Downing goes on to say that the beautiful and the picturesque (sublime) are "quite distinct, yet it by no means follows they may not be combined in landscapes [as] often seen in nature."

Weidenmann, in his work, obviously assumed Downing's definitions. By studying his plans, we see the beautiful and the picturesque created separately, and also combined. He uses gently weeping forms next to still lakes, and jagged larches next to rugged ledges, and sometimes for dramatic effect, he contrasts a rounded weeping form next to a pointed spruce or larch.

In his *Treatise*, Downing further acknowledged the influence of his friend, John Claudius Loudon (1783–1843), with whom he corresponded and whom he visited on his trip to England in 1850. Loudon, through his many writings, proposed the concept of returning gardens to these picturesque landscapes. His ideas took hold and, along with other factors, led to the intricate garden styles of the Victorian era. Many of Loudon's books were sold in America; the most notable were his *Encyclopedia of Gardening* (1822), *Encyclopedia of Plants* (1829), *The Suburban Gardener* (1828), and *The Villa Gardener* (1850).

The writings of Downing and Loudon proved a great influence on Weidenmann; their books formed the nucleus of his library, of which we regrettably do not have a listing. During this period following his arrival in New York, Weidenmann read profusely to improve his skills as a landscape architect and avidly studied the field of horticulture, especially perennials, shrubs, and trees, which he would use as part of his landscape palette. Without a doubt, Weidenmann subscribed to *The Horticulturist*, the journal that Downing published starting in 1849, three years before his death, and which continued to be printed by others for many years afterwards.

One contributor of essays to *The Horticulturist* was Eugene Achilles Baumann (1817–1869), born in the Alsace region of France, who arrived in New York on September 4, 1854, with his wife, Sofia, and five children. Baumann's reputation as a horticulturist must have preceded him because he very soon became established as a landscape gardener. The first essay he wrote for *The Horticulturist* was written in French because he had not yet mastered English (it was translated by the editors). The essay was entitled "On the Use of American Evergreen Shrubs, and of Rock Work." The thesis of the essay was to encourage Americans to use more evergreens in their landscapes, as was the trend in Europe.

It is conceivable that Weidenmann had met Baumann before each of them arrived in New York in the mid-1850s, but we have no proof. In any case, Baumann offered Weidenmann work as a landscape gardener, and they worked on many projects together, the most notable being Llewellyn Park in West Orange, New Jersey.

The park's developer, Llewellyn S. Haskell, began acquiring land in 1853, and work on the landscape began three years afterwards. Named for its developer, this was a private residential park where houses would be sited in pleasing, natural settings surrounded by landscaped grounds called "pleasure grounds." Later the term "residential park" would be used to describe such developments. The architect for this project was Alexander Jackson Davis (1803–1892), the eminent Gothic revivalist, who also owned one of the residences within the park. Davis most certainly may have had some general influence on the landscape plan, but its final articulation was by Baumann.

At the heart of the Park was a fifty acre "ramble," an intricate arrangement of curvilinear walks circulating between and around the varied topography of the ground, all of which was kept in its natural state, with some picturesque groupings of trees, shrubs, and vines added. The ramble surrounded a natural, cascading stream. The use of rambles in the landscape became a popular part of the natural landscape style in the late eighteenth century as a means of allowing people to walk through a landscape on paths laid out following the natural contours rather than on paths that were formal and symmetrical in an angular fashion. Rambles, of rustic design, were often associated with the picturesque movement of the 19th century in America. In the late 18th century they were less rustic and less undulating, and were called roundabouts, such as the ones at George Washington's "Mount Vernon" and Jefferson's "Monticello."

At the lower end of the ramble and the entrance to Llewellyn Park was the Gate Lodge, to control access to this private residential park. It was a circular structure with a steep, conical roof, its walls made of natural stone. One then entered the main drive that curved into the ramble, giving the viewer various vistas into the natural landscape. Placed on large parcels surrounding the ramble were the house sites, each having a dramatic prospect, and designed by Alexander Jackson Davis in the Gothic, bracketed Swiss, or Italian styles, which he deemed suitable to fit the natural landscape. Some of the original houses, as well as the gate house, survive.

Jacob Weidenmann was acquainted with another fellow immigrant, an Austrian named Ignaz Anton Pilat (1820–1870). Pilat was a college-trained horticulturist having taken the general course of study at the University of Vienna, and a specialized program at the University Botanical Gardens at Schonbrunn where he later worked. He is also credited with designing Prince Metternich's estate.

In 1848, revolutions were rampant in Europe, especially in Austria, so this impelled Pilat to migrate to the United States where he laid out the grounds for several estates in Georgia, perhaps the most noteworthy being the Cumming-Langdon House in Augusta. After a few years he was called back to Austria to become director of the Botanical Gardens in Vienna, but he evidently preferred life in America because he resigned his directorship in 1856 and arrived in New York within the same year as Jacob Weidenmann. It is quite possible that Weidenmann met Pilat as he toured the gardens of Europe during Weidenmann's travels there between 1853 and 1856.

Ignaz Pilat embarked on an extensive botanical survey of the Central Park land, collecting specimens and making notes. This research resulted in a 34 page pamphlet entitled *Catalogue of Plants Gathered in August and September 1857 in the Ground of Central Park.* Charles Rawolle was Pilat's official assistant on this project, but might Weidenmann have also helped as a means of learning more about botany? It is an interesting point to speculate knowing that the two were good friends.

Samuel Parsons, the eminent horticulturist and nurseryman, stated that neither Frederick Law Olmsted nor Calvert Vaux (the designers of Central Park) was a plants-man enough to work out the details of the plantings, and it was Pilat who articulated this aspect of their plans. It was also Ignaz Pilat, who was now head gardener of the Park, who oversaw all work between 1863 and 1865 when Olmsted and Vaux had resigned as landscape architects. In addition, Pilat, who had considerable talent as a designer, worked on laying out the grounds of William Cullen Bryant's estate, Cedarmere, in Roslyn, Long Island, and the Cyrus Field estate in Hastings,

New York. Field was a prominent businessman and promoter of the trans-Atlantic cable.

In addition to working with Baumann and possibly Pilat, Weidenmann also had some commissions of his own, perhaps referred to him by them. One such commission was redesigning the landscape for the estate of Robert Minturn, a wealthy merchant and clipper ship owner, in Hastings-on-Hudson, New York.

The Minturn estate was called "Locust Wood" because the residence stood in a grove of locust trees as indicated by a watercolor painting, dated about 1850. Houses in locust groves were exceedingly popular in early nineteenth century America; the groves were meant to commemorate our national hero, George Washington, who himself had planted a grove of locusts on the north side of his mansion at Mount Vernon many years before. Also, in the Hudson River Valley, the Dutch considered the locust *(Robinia pseudo-acacia)* a tree that brought good luck. By the mid-nineteenth century, however, such plantings were no longer in style, and Mr. Minturn apparently desired a picturesque landscape with a variety of trees and shrubs including evergreens, planted between curving walks and drives. Weidenmann was chosen to draw his plans.

One important commission that was certainly turned over to Weidenmann by Eugene Baumann was the design of a seventeen-lot residential park on 103 acres on Staten Island, New York. The project was known as Hill Park Estate and was "situated on the Richmond Plank Road, four-and-one-half miles from Vanderbilt's Landing, and within a short distance from the principal station of New Dorp, on the now constructing Staten Island Railroad."

The first lot and centerpiece of this subdivision had already been laid out and built according to Baumann's plans. The promotional literature for this project describes the interior of this large villa, and also its wrap-around porch, sited on a prominent rise of ground, and that the landscape "comprising about seven acres, [which] have been arranged, at considerable expense, and with the acknowledged taste, in the English style, from the designs of Mr. Ed. Baumann, Landscape gardener, and Pupil of Loudon, and they include, besides Pleasure Grounds, Lawns, Kitchen Garden, and Orchard, a lake of singular beauty stocked with Gold Fish and fed from the purest and never failing Springs." Weidenmann's plan shows a large sketch of Hill Park House in the upper corner.

The promotional literature, obviously prepared for the auction sale

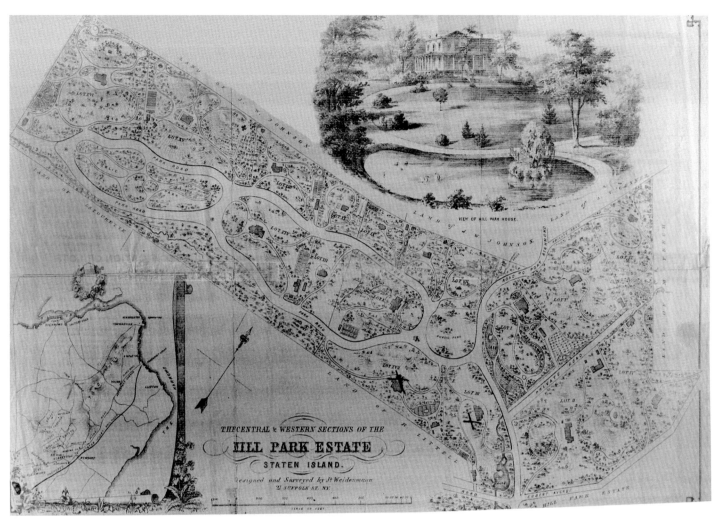

Weidenmann's presentation plan for Hill Park Estate,
Staten Island (1857).

of lots to be held on April 22, 1857, was printed on the back of Weidenmann's plan that G. W. Lewis, of 122 Fulton Street, New York, printed as a lithograph. It also states that the "remaining land of ninety-six acres, has been laid out from the designs of Mr. Weidenmann [21 Suffolk Street, New York] in the taste and form of an English Park within which a large quantity of land has been sacrificed for the purpose of forming and enclosing TWO PUBLIC PARKS for the use of the residents of Hill Park Estate." The building lots varied in size from two to nine acres.

The description of the Park continues: "the Public Parks and the broad Sidewalks and Drives of the extensive Private Roads on the Estate, furnishing that space for Rural recreation, which otherwise could not be indulged each Resident, except at the expense of the purchase and maintenance of a greater quantity of land." In other words, the lot owners would enjoy the advantages of the rural countryside without the expense of owning it.

Entrance to Hill Park was through a Ravine "of great picturesque interest," after which the road went through a valley surrounded by woods with good internal vistas. Eventually the entrance road ascended a hill that offered views to the sea. Within the Park, there were many springs and lakes adding to its overall natural beauty.

The main entrance road, situated near the east end, continued through the park, in a gently curving pattern, from south to north, and was called the Road to Port Richmond. On the east side of this road were five large lots comprising a total of thirty-four acres, each house sited on a high prospect with curved roads and paths ascending to it. Lot I, or Hill Park House, was the focal point of the section, and across the Road to Port Richmond from it was the eastern Public Park.

The remaining sixty-two acres of Hill Park contained a circular internal loop road, named Park Road. The acreage within this loop contained three lots at the east end, totaling eleven acres, and at the west end was the second public park of about four acres in size. Outside Park Road on the north side of Hill Park were seven more house lots, most of them smaller sites within the Park, five of these averaging little more than an acre, the remainder about eight acres. On the south side of Park Road loop was a thick buffer planting of trees and shrubs, except for the east end where there were two large house lots planned near the main entrance.

Each individual house site was laid out to offer privacy, all at a time when "nearer sites of Staten Island are incommoded by crowds visiting the Island from New York." The peace and healthfulness of living on the Island were strongly promoted by agents, Henry H. Leeds and Company, to the point of saying that some people who moved to the Island attained the age of ninety!

This early work of Jacob Weidenmann, executed within the few months after his arrival in America in October 1856, confirmed his ability as an accomplished artist, designer, and planner of landscapes, the field in which he chose to specialize. His early association with Eugene Baumann, and Baumann's turning over the Hill Park Estate project to him, further suggests that they may have known each other, or of each other, before Weidenmann arrived in New York.

Weidenmann's work in New York and environs enabled him to cap off his academic education with several years of practical application. It also provided steady work, which was important for his growing family. In 1860, Jacob and Anna Marguerite's daughter, Anna, was born in New York City.

*Hartford:
Public Works*

By 1860, Hartford, Connecticut, was a rapidly growing small city sixty miles inland from Long Island Sound, on the banks of the Connecticut River. Trains had recently replaced a large part of the river transport to and from the City, and many new industries emerged with the advance of technology. These ranged from James L. Howard's carriage and saddle hardware shop to Samuel Colt's firearm factory. All of these industries attracted workers from abroad, or from villages and farms in neighboring towns.

Reverend Horace Bushnell, pastor of the North Congregational Church in Hartford, led a movement to establish a city park beginning in 1853, though the idea had emerged more than twenty years earlier when a group of Hartford's citizens petitioned the Court of Common Council to "create a public square, or promenade," as public recreational spaces were called in 1827. People saw or heard about similar spaces in Europe where citizens flocked to walk and enjoy the fresh air, and where children could roll hoops and toss balls. They wanted that for Hartford, but their request failed.

Bushnell was aware of the growing industry in the city where workers toiled for long hours and lived in close quarters with no yards or gardens in which to breathe fresh air. He saw a pressing need for a large open space, an "outdoor parlor," where they could go after work or on weekends to relax a bit, to breathe fresh air, and to enjoy inspiring scenery. The park, he felt, could also act as a magnet to attract more business and industry that in turn would broaden the city's tax base. In 1850, with these concepts in mind, Bushnell selected an area of about forty acres that he thought suitable for a park, right in the center of the city of Hartford. Others with whom he talked thought the park should be sited on the outskirts of town, toward Farmington, near the present location of Nook Farm, where Samuel Clemens (Mark Twain) and Harriet Beecher Stowe were to later build their houses. Bushnell said that it should be near the central buzz of the city where people could readily see it and use it, and where visitors who came by train could see it like a jewel in a crown as they entered town.

Based on these principles, Reverend Bushnell drew his own conceptual plan for a proposed park to be sited in a shallow valley a few hundred yards from Hartford's Main Street. Few would have selected this site because of its swampy ground and ramshackle houses, outhouses, and pig sties, along with a tannery, soap factory, and grist mill. It also included the yard and some tracks of the

New Haven and Hartford Railroad. The mills, which generated considerable pollution and stench, were along the Little River, then called the Hog River.

Bushnell could see through all of this unsightly development and erase it from his mind, envisioning a large tract of sloping ground, along a cleaned-up river, where citizens could take walks, children could play, and businessmen could make deals as they strolled with their clients. Everyone, rich and poor, could breathe fresh air, and in turn, the park would upgrade the image of the city, and promote further desirable development.

On September 5, 1853, the Court of Common Council reluctantly allowed Reverend Bushnell to appear before them to present his plan (some members thought his idea frivolous). After his long and carefully crafted presentation, the minds of many Councilmen began to change, and by the December 12 meeting that year, the Council voted to proceed with the park concept. At this time, however, the Council had no established legal powers for acquiring land by eminent domain for public use. Working behind the scenes through influential acquaintances, Bushnell was able to have the Council's charter revised to enable them to do so.

According to a careful estimate, acquiring the various parcels of land comprising the forty-acre tract would require over one hundred thousand dollars, so on January 5, 1854, the citizens of Hartford were invited to the polls to see if they would authorize the expenditure of $105,000 dollars for the park project (equivalent to over two million dollars today). The response was overwhelmingly in favor, 1,687 to 683, almost a three to one margin. Soon, parcel by parcel, the land was acquired, but the process would last almost four years. It was a rough road before the last piece was obtained, with all kinds of hurdles. One of them was a petition brought to the Council by a certain faction that even included some Council members, to abandon the whole project, sell off the land already acquired at a good profit, and buy a new and cheaper tract in the area of the famed Charter Oak, nearer the edge of the City. Fortunately, after considerable haggling and political maneuvering, the latter scheme failed. Hartford's new park would go down in history as the first public park in the United States built entirely with public funds.

As the acquisition of the last remaining sites was nearing completion in late 1857, the newly appointed Park Committee, chaired by James L. Howard, decided to announce a competition for the design of the park, just as New York was doing for its proposed Central Park.

Prizes of three hundred and two hundred dollars would be awarded for the first and second place winners. Twelve contestants applied, and on July 12, 1858, the winners were announced.

First prize was awarded to Gervaise Wheeler, a British-born designer who lived in New York, and the second place winner was Seth Marsh, the city engineer. Wheeler's plan was declared too costly to implement, so Marsh was asked to take desirable aspects of each plan and combine them into a composite. As is often the case with such actions, a cumbersome product evolved, one that was not exactly to Marsh's "[taste] in all respects, but endeavoring to incorporate in it as much as possible, the ideas of some of our most interested citizens." About a year after this effort, Thomas McClunie, one of the other contestants, claimed that " ideas furnished by me for the layout of the Park" were utilized in Marsh's composite plan. The Park Committee voted not to argue the point, and they awarded a second place prize to McClunie as well.

There was dissatisfaction with Marsh's conglomerate plan and the way work was beginning on the site. The ground, after basic clearing was done, was being graded with little regard for the natural flow of contours, or for what would please the eye. The plan itself lacked harmony, which it needed to unify the two parts of the park separated by Bliss Street (now Trinity Street); these two sections seemed like two separate parks. Not only did the walks curve through the site in an awkward manner, but also the trees were placed along these walks in straight lines, rather than in picturesque or natural groupings. Bushnell and the newly formed Board of Park Commissioners could see that the plan was not working and something needed to be done.

The new Park Board, appointed on May 28, 1860, decided that a professional landscape architect (called landscape gardener then) was needed in order to devise a workable, harmonious, artistic, yet practical plan, as well as to superintend its implementation. They began searching for a candidate, but during that era few were qualified. On July 17, 1860, the Board, consisting of president William Collins, George Beach, James L. Howard, Gordon Bissell, and Charles Pond (soon replaced by Gustavus F. Davis), interviewed Jacob Weidenmann. It is interesting to consider how they heard about this recent immigrant who had been practicing landscape architecture for less than four years in the environs of New York.

In one of her two written sketches about her father, Marguerite Weidenmann, his youngest daughter, states that ". . . he made the acquaintance of some persons who were interested in bringing him to Hartford . . . notably a Mr. Niles." Niles is believed to have been Jonathan Sands Niles (1804–1878), a native of Shaftsbury, Vermont. With his brother, Ebenezer, he eventually migrated to Cincinnati, Ohio where they established the Niles and Company Tool Plant and produced machinery such as engine-operated sugar mills to replace horse-powered equipment for the sugar refining industry in Louisiana. Jonathan Sands Niles retired from this business in 1858, at which time he moved to Hartford, Connecticut, where he built a fine home at 60 Farmington Avenue.

Jacob Weidenmann had a Cincinnati connection in Adolph Strauch (1822–1883), a practicing landscape gardener. Strauch was a native of the province of Silesia in Prussia, and in 1851, after more than ten years of apprenticing in horticulture and landscape gardening in Vienna, Schoenbrun, Luxenburg, Berlin, Hamburg, The Hague, Amsterdam, Ghent, Paris, and finally London, he decided to migrate to the United States in 1851. His proficiency in German, English, French, Polish and Bohemian had enabled him to serve as a guide at the great London Exhibition of 1851.

By 1852, Adolph Strauch was well situated in Cincinnati, designing estates for the wealthy. Of all his extensive projects there, he is most remembered for his design of Spring Grove Cemetery, which, according to his friend Frederick Law Olmsted was ". . . the best cemetery in the United States."

During the latter years of Strauch's apprenticeships in various European cities, Jacob Weidenmann was also traveling about and visiting many of the same places. It is presumed that the two had met, and that they renewed their acquaintance when they both found themselves in America a few years later. Weidenmann was in contact with Strauch in Cincinnati, perhaps to assist him, because Strauch was rapidly building a practice not just in Ohio but also in Michigan, Illinois, Tennessee, and elsewhere. Weidenmann designed at least one major estate in Cincinnati for which there is documentation.

Without a doubt, Jonathan Sands Niles either met Jacob Weidenmann when he went to Cincinnati, or heard about his capabilities from Adolph Strauch, so that when he arrived in Hartford he told his new neighbors, George Beach and James Howard, about him. Both gentlemen served on the newly formed Park Board.

Many years later, on April 8, 1901, John Olmsted, the adopted son and actual nephew of Frederick Law Olmsted, wrote that it was his father who recommended Jacob Weidenmann to the Park Board. The elder Olmsted, residing in New York at that time, had a strong interest in his native Hartford and corresponded with Rev. Horace Bushnell, the chief promoter of the new park. No doubt Olmsted had met Weidenmann in New York, especially if Weidenmann assisted Ignatz Pilat on the plant inventory for New York's Central Park.

What John Olmsted did not report is that his father had been approached by the Hartford Park Committee to see if he would design the proposed City Park. The *Hartford Courant* reported on June 3, 1858: "It is suggested that Frederick Law Olmsted, a native of this city, who has lately been chosen to superintend the laying out of the large Park in New York, would be a proper person to give shape to the result of our modest enterprise. We presume Olmsted, if he would consent to undertake it, would do as well as anyone who could be named, now that we have no longer a Downing in the land."

We do not know which of these two stories is authentic. Perhaps both Niles and Frederick Law Olmsted suggested Weidenmann for the job of park superintendent, which would have strengthened his credentials. In any case, on the same day as the interview, Weidenmann was offered the position, and on the next day, July 18, 1860, the Park Board offered him a contract which he signed. It stated that he ". . . be employed as Superintendent of the Park for the purpose of laying out the same including surveying, making necessary plans, planting and selecting trees, etc., making estimates of cost, etc., employing and superintending laborers, etc., under the direction of the Commissioners, at a salary of $600.00 per annum." The first job assigned to Weidenmann was to make ". . . accurate surveys and plans for drainage and to lay out the ground with a working plan showing walks, planting, and other improvements."

From the list of Weidenmann's new duties cited in his contract, it is obvious that the Park Commissioners knew of his expertise and capabilities, from site engineering and construction to horticulture and art, and they also had confidence in his ability to manage and supervise laborers. Nonetheless, it was a very delicate situation for Weidenmann, because he not only had to produce a new plan that everyone would like and that would fit the budget, one that would please Bushnell, the Park Board, and the Common Council, but he also had to correct the work that had been done incorrectly, and appease the workmen who had done it.

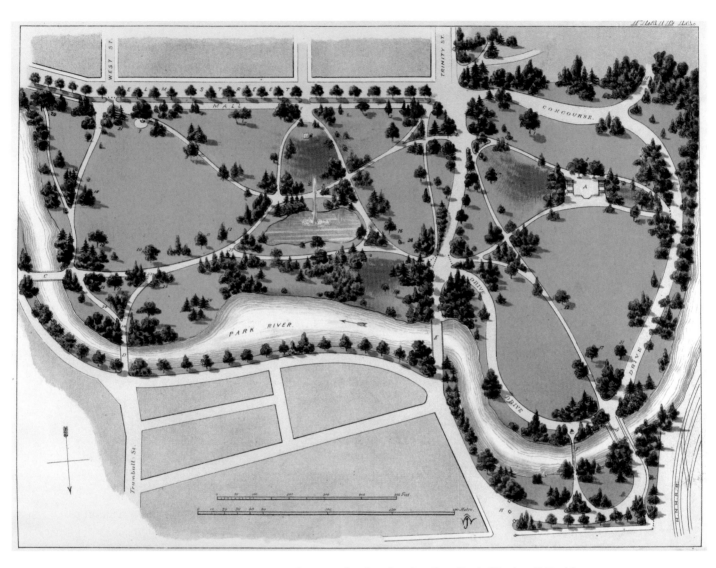

Weidenmann's plan for the City Park (Bushnell Park).
From *Beautifying Country Homes*.

Jacob Weidenmann was eager to start. He moved his wife and young daughter Anna into a rented house at 4 Summer Street, just four blocks from the new park site. These must have been temporary quarters because within the next year, the family was renting a house from Trinity College, which at that time was adjacent to the park on the south side.

Soon Weidenmann produced a new plan. It was based on the concept first put forth by Bushnell in 1853, of a picturesque landscape, done in a natural style, like so many of the parks surrounding the large manor houses in England and on the Continent that were influenced by the early work of William Kent, Lancelot Brown, and Humphry Repton, as previously mentioned. Bridges were to connect the park over the river at places where city streets met the park, so that people could walk to the park, cross over these bridges, and then stroll along the curving paths within.

The system of curving walks and drives combined with undulating topography provided a perfect place for people to stroll and enjoy the surroundings. In addition, as we study the original plan, we can see that the long, curving walks had a strong east-west sweep and thus unified the two separate parts of the park separated by Trinity Street. Weidenmann even curved Trinity Street slightly, and made it part of a peripheral carriage drive in the west end of the park as a further unifying device.

Access to the park from the central city was over the various foot-bridges as well as over the dam and cascade, all features that were shown in both the conceptual Bushnell plan as well as the Marsh composite. In fact, the dam-cascade (opposite High Street) had already been built when Weidenmann assumed his duties. On the south side of the park, where there was no river, Weidenmann emphasized the entrances to the park, opposite the side streets, with small plazas, and the curving walks radiated from these.

Walks also defined and outlined the green spaces and directed visitors to various focal features. For example, from the small plaza opposite Clinton Street on the south side, the two walks enclose a green lawn that terminated with a fountain pool in the center of the park, and from the pool as the visitor looked back, a statue of Rev. Horace Bushnell was planned. The pool and the statue were the two focal points of the east end of the park. As the main focus on the south end, Weidenmann projected a stone terrace on the highest point in the park from which various events as well as the views beyond could be observed. The terrace was also designed

City Park (Bushnell Park), Hartford, Connecticut, shortly after its completion in the late 1860s, showing one of the connecting bridges to the city center.

to be a stand for speakers and musical events, and built into its wall was a fountain; beneath the terrace floor was a storage basement. This stone terrace was built in 1865, and it was reminiscent of the Praeneste that William Kent had designed at Rousham House, Oxfordshire, England, over a century earlier.

To further make the two sections of the park read as one, Weidenmann created a wide plaza just over the Park River Bridge leading to Trinity Street from which several walks and the carriage drive radiated into the park. It was near this point where the City had architect George Keller build the magnificent Soldiers and Sailors Memorial Arch in 1884–1886, long after Weidenmann had left Hartford, though we can be certain that Weidenmann would have approved of it as another unifying and focal element.

Weidenmann drew his planting plan to achieve several goals. Picturesque plantings were planned to define the various spaces in the park delineated by the walk system. By so doing, the vastness of forty acres was scaled down into smaller, humanized spaces. The plantings were also arranged to frame vistas, to emphasize focal points, to create illusions, or to direct pedestrian flow. In other words, the walks and the plantings worked in concert to strengthen the entire plan. Once the general location of the plantings was decided, Jacob Weidenmann applied his artistry and horticultural knowledge to create variation in color, texture, and form, by juxtaposing evergreens and deciduous trees and shrubs, using coarse leaved catalpas and fine-needled cypress to create interest, sweet gums to produce purple color in the autumn, and Lombardy Poplars for exotic form and shimmering foliage. These plant forms are clearly evident on his plan rendering.

Reverend Horace Bushnell and the Park Commissioners were pleased with Weidenmann's plan, finished in the late winter of 1861. On March 20 of that year, William L. Collins (1812–1865), chairman of the Park Commissioners, distributed an invitation that read:

> The Park Commissioners would be pleased to have you call at the Store of Collins Brothers and Co., this week, and examine the Plan of City Park, just finished by Mr. Weidenman, Park Superintendent.

The citizens of Hartford were pleased with the proposed plan and were eager to have the work proceed as soon as possible. In Weidenmann's own words:

> The grounds when first begun were to a large extent a swamp and settled with rude shanties–an unhealthy, desolate

place . . . . The drainage of the grounds having been entirely neglected, this work was systematically laid out and a map of all drains and underground surface water was [prepared]. Expensive alterations on the east and west parks, the correction of the river, the building of bridges, the construction of roads and walks, the grading, filling, and planting, progressed as the financial appropriations made by the City Council would allow. The main portion of the park is undulating, a condition produced by artificial means. It is about ten feet above the level of the river, though the south-west part is a natural hill about sixty feet high, from which a pretty view can be obtained.

Two years later, in 1863, there were still paths and roads to finish, some of the lawns to complete, and the skating pond with fountain were still under construction; however, enough of the paths were done so that thirty cast iron benches were purchased to place along them in order to satisfy Hartford's anxious citizens.

A view of the completed City Park (Bushnell Park), c. 1870.

Work progressed apace, the stone terrace was built, the walks, lawns, and plantings completed, and by April 1, 1870, Hartford could boast about its new park. The project cost a total of $337,031.08 (about five million dollars in today's currency), a large sum for those times, but as Mayor Chapman reported: "When we consider that here for all time is preserved for the public use for the enjoyment of all, then cost is seen to be really small compared with the benefits conferred by this crowning beauty of the city."

Obviously, Jacob Weidenmann was pleased with the progress of the park, though it is certain that his patience was taxed because progress depended upon the availability of funds which were appropriated incrementally. But he was able to see the work to completion, and during those years, two more daughters were born to the Weidenmann family, Elise in 1861, and Marguerite in 1868.

It was not many years after completion that the Park was threatened by intrusion. In the early 1870s, there was talk of constructing a new capitol building, and suggestions were made to build it in the new park. Bushnell was appalled, and he even had Weidenmann draw a plan to site the building elsewhere. After much discussion and haggling, the city fathers were convinced that they should persuade Trinity College to move their campus, and that the City Council should agree to purchase the College's original site and build the new state capitol there. There was considerable negotiation regarding price, though a deal was soon made, and the new capitol building was built where it sits today. The first legislative session was held there on November 26, 1878.

Over the years, many features such as statues and planting beds were added to Bushnell Park, so that by the end of the nineteenth century, though the park still retained its original ground plan, it looked more Victorian in that many intricate flower beds were built along the walks and the river. Another major feature added to the park, in addition to the Soldiers and Sailors Memorial Arch of 1884–86, was the elegant Corning Fountain of 1899.

The completed City Park, circa 1870.

Throughout the nineteenth century and into the twentieth, the park was meticulously cared for; however, after the First World War, and particularly during the Depression of 1929, maintenance began to decline, and the park eventually fell into neglect after World War II. Further changes occurred after the disastrous floods of 1936, when the Park River was put underground, leaving only the skating pond. In 1959, the Connecticut Highway Department threatened to place a connector between the present Interstates 84 and 91, through the park, a threat that kept resurfacing on and off for twenty years.

In 1981, the Bushnell Park Foundation was organized by a group of interested citizens to assist the City of Hartford in providing care and oversight for the park. They and the city realized that they have a jewel, one that should be carefully preserved. Jacob Weidenmann took great pride in this park, his first successful public project.

Cedar Hill Cemetery

As Bushnell Park was being built, Hartford's leaders were enjoying their reputation in the forefront of the public park movement. Some of the same park proponents, however, realized that Hartford was lagging behind by not having a rural cemetery. The Boston area had already had Mount Auburn Cemetery in Cambridge for over thirty years, and even small towns like Mystic Bridge, Connecticut, already had rural cemeteries. Hartford must work towards having one also, its leaders felt.

Rural cemeteries were burial grounds laid in a natural, park-like setting rather than row-on-row, as in churchyards. In 1846, Andrew Jackson Downing wrote an essay on the subject in his journal, *The Horticulturist:*

> The great attraction of these cemeteries, to the mass of the community, is not in the fact that they are burial places, or

solemn places of meditation for the friends of the deceased, or striking exhibitions of monumental sculpture, though all these have their influence. All these might be realized in a burial ground, planted with straight lines of willows, and somber avenues of evergreens. The true secret of the attractions lies in the natural beauty of the sites and in the tasteful and harmonious embellishment of these sites by art. Nearly all these cemeteries were rich portions of forest land, broken by hill and dale, and varied by copses and glades, like Mount Auburn and Greenwood [in Brooklyn, NY], or old country seats, richly wooded with fine planted trees, like Laurel Hill [Philadelphia]. Hence, to an inhabitant of the town, a visit to one of these spots has the united charm of nature and art— the double wealth of rural and moral associations. It awakens at the same moment, the feeling of human sympathy and the love of natural beauty, implanted in every heart. His must be a dull or trifling soul that neither swells with emotion, nor rises with admiration, at the varied beauty of these hallowed spots.

In 1863, a group of gentlemen in Hartford organized for the purpose of establishing a rural cemetery in their fast-growing city. They elected Dr. James C. Jackson to be their secretary, and William Collins their chairman. Collins, it will be recalled, was the first chairman of the Board of Park Commissioners. One of the group's first tasks was to select a site for the cemetery, so a sub-committee was appointed consisting of Dr. Jackson and Hiram Bissell, and they asked landscape architect Jacob Weidenmann, Superintendent of the City Park to join them. Obviously these gentlemen were pleased with Weidenmann's work on the park and wanted the same expert advice with their new project. Four sites were visited and studied and finally one was chosen.

While the site selection committee was searching, the cemetery committee had to organize legally, so they petitioned the Connecticut General Assembly for a charter and act of incorporation, which they received in May of 1864. By June of the following year, the Cemetery Board was officially organized with the following members: Henry A. Parker, William Hungerford, Charles Cheney, Austin C. Dunham, William T. Lee, Jonathan S. Niles, George Beach, Calvin Day, Albert Day, Gordon Trumbull, Marshall Jewell, Pliny Jewell, Jr., Stiles D. Sperry, Thomas Belknap, Dr. James C. Jackson, and William R. Cone, all prominent and prosperous Hartford businessmen and professionals.

Now that the Cedar Hill Cemetery Association was officially chartered, land acquisition could actually begin for the selection committee's recommended site. There were nine parcels in the 268 acre composite tract, and four of them had to be obtained by eminent domain. One of the largest tracts was the old Hillhouse farm. The land acquisition process took about one year, and during this time, Jacob Weidenmann, was asked by the new Cemetery Board to draw a conceptual plan.

The new rural cemetery site had all of the attributes the selection committee placed high on its list. It was sufficiently removed from the center of Hartford by about three miles, possessed suitable soil for burials, and had:

> the largest variety of surface, beauty of landscape, and running water . . . [and was] charmingly diversified with vale, lawn, forest, picturesque rocks, stately shade trees, running and pond water, and altogether remarkably adapted to beautification, the highest point on the western boundary being 173 feet above the New Haven Turnpike [eastern boundary].

The site ascended gradually from the New Haven Turnpike (now Fairfield Avenue) to a westerly ridge referred to as Hillhouse Ridge because it had been part of the Hillhouse farm. Then the land sloped into a gentle valley before ascending to another ridge near the westernmost boundary. On these ridges grew cedars, hence the name of the cemetery, first called Cedar Mountain Cemetery, but soon changed to Cedar Hill. From these ridges there were distant views north to the City of Hartford, and also the Holyoke Range in Massachusetts, sixty miles away. In a northwesterly direction, Mount Tom was visible in the Berkshires of Massachusetts, and to the east and south, the viewer could see the plains along the Connecticut River with Glastonbury beyond.

The water on the site, though desirable, posed a major problem because it consisted of brooks and pools in a marshy setting. This wetland was mostly in the twenty-eight acres of the site that were located in Hartford; the other 240 acres were mostly located in Wethersfield, with some in Newington. This situation was the only drawback of the site, and it would be a challenge to Jacob Weidenmann. He had to create a pleasing and impressive entrance through this swampy land because it would not be acceptable to have the entrance to Hartford's new rural cemetery in another town.

Weidenmann proposed draping a verdant lawn over the rolling

Reservoir Lake, Cedar Hill Cemetery,
showing the main entrance drive in the background.
From *Beautifying Country Homes*.

terrain, and reserving as many of the natural features as possible. The site's natural landscape with its rocks, water, and trees, would be complemented with gently curving roads and paths for access, making certain that their placement did not conflict with the natural contours. He then planned that sections of ground between these roads and paths would be sensitively divided into burial lots, leaving ample room between them for trees, while the backgrounds of the lots themselves would be enriched by shrub plantings. Each lot would be marked with a simple monument, with individual graves marked with stones flush with the ground.

This concept was actually an adaptation of the natural landscape style advanced by William Kent, Lancelot Brown, and others mentioned earlier, and also expressed by Thomas Whately in his *Modern Gardening,* published in London in 1778, in which he said:

> Nature, always simple, employs but four materials in the composition of her scenes, ground, wood, water, and rocks. The cultivation of nature has introduced a fifth species, the buildings requisite for the accommodation of men. Each of these admits of a variety of figure, dimensions, colour, and situation. Every landskip [landscape] is composed of these parts only; every beauty in a landskip depends on the application of their several varieties.

In the "open lawn system" of cemetery design, as Weidenmann called his concept, the monuments and service buildings were the "buildings" referred to in Whately's quote, and the rest of the landscape must be tastefully articulated by manipulating the natural terrain as a backdrop. No fences, walls, or curbs would be allowed, for they would interrupt the natural. In fact, though Weidenmann strongly recommended flat grave markers so as not to impede the natural eye flow over the landscape, this concept was almost impossible to enforce over time.

An important part of the open lawn plan was an ornamental fore-ground. Weidenmann wrote: "An imposing landscape scenery in a rural cemetery creates dignity, and produces that degree of grandeur to which the place is destined." By an "imposing landscape" he meant vast stretches of lawn or grassland, with copses of trees informally composed, along with some single specimen trees placed strategically here and there to frame vistas or to stand as focal points. He then went on: ". . . the largest part of the ornamental grounds shall be at the main approach or entrance to the cemetery, where display of beautiful landscape views will produce the best results." With "best results" Weidenmann meant the creation of a

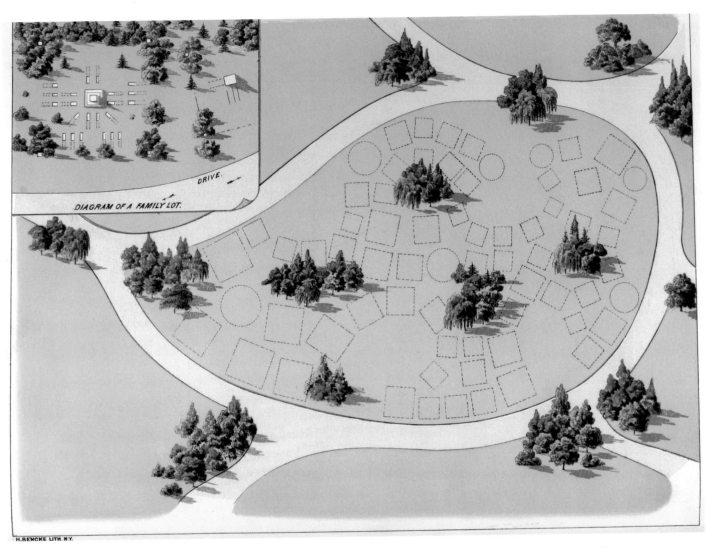

DIAGRAM OF A FAMILY LOT.

DRIVE.

H.BENCKE LITH. N.Y.

Typical plot layout for the open lawn concept of cemetery design.
From *Beautifying Country Homes*.

peaceful ambiance so that the visitor, by passing through, would be struck by the peacefulness and reach a serene frame of mind for his visit. One other major element that Weidenmann considered of utmost importance to complete the foreground landscape was the inclusion of a body, or bodies, of water, an element that always creates intense interest in a landscape and also contributes significantly to a peaceful and serene scene. He summed up this point by saying: "A landscape without water is imperfect, no matter how beautiful otherwise it may be."

Jacob Weidenmann developed a plan that created an ornamental foreground where he concentrated the water of the swampy area into five lakes, two small, two medium, and one large, and then he interconnected them. The visitor to the cemetery would pass through the proposed gate house and then proceed over a long, slightly curved avenue over a dam with a water cascade between the two sections of Cedar Lake. Proceeding, the visitor would find Nyssa Lake (later named Lynn Mawr) on the left. This, the largest lake, spanned eight acres, and was fed by a brook that flowed from Reservoir Pond in the distance over a series of man-made cascades. There were to be swan houses on two islands in Nyssa Lake for which Weidenmann drew plans. Weidenmann had no problems convincing the Committee that the remaining fifty acres in the ornamental foreground that were not consumed by lakes were to remain free of burials because the soil had a high water table. By leaving this area grassland, with appropriate plantings around the lakes, a peaceful and natural ornamental foreground was created. As visitors traveled the one-third mile along Inway Avenue, as the new entrance road was named, the quiet surroundings put them in a serene frame of mind simply to meditate or to mourn their loved ones.

Before Weidenmann began planning, he had his friend, Adolph Strauch, come to Hartford from Cincinnati, for a day's consultation. Weidenmann knew of Strauch's creation of a grand ornamental foreground in Spring Grove Cemetery in Cincinnati, complete with lakes and fountains in a beautifully landscaped lawn of several acres, designed to complement his open lawn scheme within the Cemetery. We have no details of this consultation, but surely the complicated foreground area for Cedar Hill was discussed.

None of Weidenmann's plans for Cedar Hill have been found except for a color rendering of the proposed scheme. This plan was for two-and-one-half acres of the cemetery, and it was drawn to show the arrangement of the curving drives and paths, with burial lots between them. The placement of trees in the ample ground

ELEVATION.

CROSS-SECTION through A.B.

PLAN.

SCALE of ELEVATION & CROSS-SECTION

SCALE of PLAN.

SCALE of DETAILS.

Weidenmann's plan for a swan house at Cedar Hill to be built at the edge of the lake. From *American Garden Architecture*.

Weidenmann's presentation rendering of Cedar Mountain Cemetery (Cedar Hill).

between the lots, using shrubs as background for the monuments, is carefully depicted, as is ample tree buffering around the perimeter of the Cemetery. The rendering clearly shows a ten-foot lawn buffer on each side of the roads through the grounds, a concept further strengthening the open lawn scheme. Weidenmann shows a major monument in each lot, with the flat markers for the graves. Mausolea were sited along the distant hill and in a group. While he was adamantly opposed to curbs, fences, or walls around burial lots, he does show a few so designed in the lower right of the rendering, and it is assumed that he did this to show contrast with his fine open lawn system, and how much better that system would be. This rendering was obviously used as a presentation piece to inform the Cemetery Board of his ideas. In his book, *Beautifying Country Homes,* he wrote:

> Instead of having each lot ornamented within its own boundary, we lay out little lawns or recesses in such a way that every lot adjoining each one has the benefit of it; by this arrangement the entire section presents a very pleasing appearance.

It is interesting to compare the Cedar Hill rendering with Weidenmann's rendering of Bushnell Park. They both feature the natural landscape, with curved and flowing walks and drives working in concert with the natural contours, with plenty of green lawn between them, all enhanced with trees, shrubs, and bodies of water. The major difference between the two is that in Bushnell Park the lawn areas are for play and relaxation, while at Cedar Hill they are for burials. When we consider that the park movement in the United States was an outgrowth of the rural cemetery movement, this similarity is not difficult to understand.

While none of Jacob Weidenmann's working drawings are extant, we are fortunate to have several of his designs for the Cedar Hill drainage system, drainage outlets, the pond bed construction, a plan for the cascade and overflow for the lakes, and a large plan that shows the arrangement of graves within burial lots, and how these burial areas should be landscaped. These details, taken from his plans, were used to illustrate sections of the book that he wrote a few years afterwards called *Beautifying Country Homes* (1870).

By the work season of 1865, eighty laborers were building the entrance road, configuring the ornamental foreground, and laying out the first six sections of the Cemetery beyond the foreground. By July of 1866, one year later, three-and-three-fifths miles of road had been built, including the entrance road, which traversed the

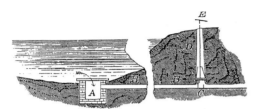

Typical construction details for Cedar Hill Cemetery. From *Beautifying Country Homes*.

dam and cascade between the lakes. Most of the soil dug from the lakes was used to build the dam and as a base for some of the roads.

On June 24, 1868, the Cemetery was formally consecrated. Rev. J. H. Twichell, the recently appointed pastor of the Asylum Hill Congregational Church, gave the invocation. A major historical address, entitled "I Will Not Live Always," was presented by Rowland Swift, Esquire, a prominent Hartford banker and member of the Board, and the entire program of talks, reading from the scriptures, and singing of hymns, was terminated by an invocation by Reverend Francis Goodwin. Weidenmann was serving as Cedar Hill Cemetery's first superintendent. At this time he had the distinction of being superintendent of Hartford's first park and its first rural cemetery.

In the last quarter of the nineteenth century, in addition to the continued expansion of the Cemetery grounds, several buildings were added. A house for the superintendent was completed in 1880. Shortly afterwards, in 1882, the Northam Chapel was built. In 1889, the Gallup Memorial Gateway was added, consisting of two fine granite buildings, one an office, the other a waiting room, flanking an elaborate entrance gate. George Keller (1842–1935), who during the same decade designed the Soldiers and Sailors Memorial Arch for Bushnell Park, designed the Chapel and gateway buildings. All of these structures form an impressive complex at the entrance of the Cemetery.

Jacob Weidenmann had proposed his own design for an entrance gate for Cedar Hill prior to Keller's plans. It was a complex structure, in the Swiss-rustic style, complete with bell-tower. This design had originally been made for the State Asylum for the Insane, in Concord, New Hampshire, and then "modified," by removing the bell tower, for Cedar Hill, but the Board did not accept the design.

Cedar Hill Cemetery still retains its basic open lawn plan, and it is a virtual arboretum because of its collection of trees and shrubs, many of which date from the nineteenth century. Two of the lakes are gone in the ornamental foreground, but the foreground is still preserved as a serene entry to the Cemetery. The entrance road, which traverses the dam along the lakes was restored in 2004, and the original drainage designed by Weidenmann and laid by his crew was replaced after having served for 144 years, a tribute to Weidenmann's expertise. During the years of the 20th Century, when lots were laid out in the vale between the two ridges, the open lawn scheme was not followed as previously in that the graves were placed row-upon- row; however, new sections of the cemetery, especially those added in the 1990s, have returned to Weidenmann's original scheme.

Cedar Hill Cemetery today.

Cedar Hill's spacious roads follow natural contours.

Entrance to Cedar Hill Cemetery.   Hartford Conn.

The entrance gate complex at
Cedar Hill Cemetery. Starting
at the left: Chapel, waiting
room, gate, office (all designed
by George Keller, architect),
and the superintendent's house.

Weidenmann's design for the
entrance gate, Cedar Hill
Cemetery, not adopted.
Plan was originally made for
the Asylum for the Insane,
Concord, New Hampshire.

At the south end of Hartford's Main Street is a triangular green,
a relic of Hartford's original plan dating back to the 1630s.
In the 1860s it was one of only three public spaces in Hartford, the
new City Park and State House Square being the others. As was
the fate of so many greens and commons in the 19th Century,
their original size was being cut away by wagons taking short cuts
and encroaching upon them. As early as 1816, the Court of Common
Council voted to have Messrs. Michael Olcott and James Ward
"designate the lines [boundaries] of the Green so that it might be
fenced." The Green was fenced that same year, and cattle and horses
belonging to neighboring residents were allowed to graze within, a
common practice during these times as a means of mowing the grass.

The new fence around South Green lasted for about twenty years,
typical of wooden fences, so in 1837 Bristol and Wharton of Dutch
Point erected a new fence. A few years afterwards, the Common
Council was petitioned to "do something to prevent horses and
cattle from getting into the enclosure and destroying and damaging
the shrubbery." Some attempt had been made to beautify the
Green, and by 1851, eleven shade trees were planted there.

Residents surrounding the Green and other Hartford citizens
passing through the area were constantly complaining about the
condition of the Green, so in 1868, the Court of Common Council
placed the care of the Green, as well as the State House grounds,
under the supervision of the Park Commission, and it is believed
that Jacob Weidenmann drew his plan for improving South Green
at this time.

The triangular Green (outlined by Wyllys Avenue at its base, with
Maple and Wethersfield Avenues bordering its other two sides),
needed to be defined in order to keep its thirteen and one-half acres
from eroding away more. Weidenmann proposed a granite curb
around it, and within the curbed area a wide lawn strip, planted
with alternating Norway and Sugar Maples to provide shade for a
peripheral walk. For the apex of the Green, he planned a circular
plaza with a stone bench where people could sit and look down
the center to a large pool and fountain, the main focus of the whole
Green. This apex plaza was oriented around a large, existing elm
tree, which provided accent as well as needed shade.

Additional walks radiated from the central fountain plaza to the
outer peripheral walk. The plaza itself was paved with gravel and left

large enough to serve as a play area for children. The Green's internal walks were also gravel, and picturesque groupings of trees and shrubs, rich in texture and varied in form, were designated surrounding the central plaza and defining the entrances to the Green. Spruces, cypresses, pines, and flowering trees and shrubs were proposed. The areas between the walks were left as open lawn for recreation and special events, with only a few shrub groupings along the outer edges to break monotonous visual lines.

Weidenmann's plan was not immediately implemented. In fact, on March 9, 1868, the New York Circus was given permission to set up on the Green, and the following year residents complained to the Council that during that event, the partially rotting fence was "carried away," and that trees (those planted in 1851) had been severely damaged. The Council responded that there would be no more expenditures on the South Green until "a substantial fence is installed," and the Green curbed and guttered. Residents continued to apply pressure upon the Council, and in 1870, it declared that South Green "has for a long time been in a condition which was not only discreditable to the city, but which rendered it a positive nuisance to those in the vicinity." The Council then authorized the expenditure of $6,650 (about $99,000 today) to build an iron fence and construct a curb around the Green. A year later, the Park Commissioners reported that the Green was being regraded and walks installed.

Much of Weidenmann's plan was implemented in the 1870s, and for a decade thereafter, the Green enjoyed a period of opulence. In fact, in 1898, its name was changed to Barnard Park in honor of Henry Barnard, Connecticut's first Commissioner of Education, and also the United States' first Commissioner of Education, appointed in 1867. He lived in the South Green neighborhood at one time. To most people, however, it is still known as South Green. During the twentieth century, the Green had its ups and downs, and today Hartford residents still complain about its condition.

There was much interest in the landscape of Hartford during this post-Civil War period. Cedar Hill Cemetery was now established, the City Park was all but complete, and South Green, as well as the Statehouse Grounds had been refurbished, all under Weidenmann's guidance. On the avenues radiating from the city, elegant houses were being constructed with richly planted landscapes that, along with the many trees planted along these avenues, would make the entire city a virtual park. A few years later, when Mark Twain built his mansion on Farmington Avenue, he would declare: "Of all the beautiful towns it has been my fortune to see, this is the chief."

Weidenmann's plan for South Green.
From *Beautifying Country Homes*.

Chapter Three

Hartford: Private Commissions

In 1843, Dr. John Simpkins Butler was appointed superintendent of the Hartford Retreat for the Insane. Butler came to his ancestral Hartford after eighteen years of study and private practice. He was born in Northampton, Massachusetts, where his father had settled after leaving Hartford, and where his ancestors had been among the original settlers in 1636. Dr. Butler studied at Yale College, and following graduation, he took a series of courses in medicine at Harvard College, and also at Jefferson Medical College in Philadelphia, receiving his medical degree in 1829. In that year, he opened an office for the practice of medicine in Worcester, Massachusetts, where he practiced for ten years.

In Worcester, Butler became interested in patients with mental illness, the field in which he decided to specialize. Soon he became director of the new Boston Lunatic Hospital, a position he held for three years before returning to private practice in Boston. His particular interest in mental health, however, prompted him to take the position as superintendent of the Retreat in Hartford.

The Retreat was founded in 1822, twenty-one years before Butler arrived. There was a very large complex of buildings, all connected, on the Washington Street side of the grounds, now called the Central Building. Behind it to the east was a large thirty-seven acre expanse of land, much of it "rough, and a broad swale of low land extended through the center of the lot, most of the year wet and always impassable, especially for ladies; it was of little use, except for grass and a distant view. Many of the trees were crowded and interfering with one another and most of the planting had originally been made without a systematic plan."

Dr. Butler strongly believed that natural beauty was "an important element in successful treatment of Insanity," and he wanted a "therapeutic Arcadia" where he could ramble "with patients about the embellished grounds, and wax poetic about flowers—the 'best of medicine'—and hold parties on the green." He would invite the public to see " these pleasant changes so that they would be disabused that an asylum was repulsive."

With this premise in mind, Dr. Butler hired Hartford native, Frederick Law Olmsted and his partner Calvert Vaux, to produce a plan to improve this wasteland behind the main Central Building. These gentlemen were both enjoying renown, as well as suffering some headaches, over their recent award-winning plan for Central Park in New York. They had also been awarded some other commissions, but they found time to go to Hartford in 1860 to commence work on the plan, which they completed for presentation in the spring of 1861. The plan was well received by the Retreat Board, and arrangements were made to proceed with the project.

The plan was in the English natural landscape style, with a strong buffer of natural plantings around the entire perimeter of the property, specifically along Maple Avenue to the east, Retreat Avenue to the north, and Washington Street on the west. The southern boundary, also thickly planted, separated the Retreat grounds from neighbors on the south, property acquired later. Within this heavy buffer planting consisting of a mixture of evergreens and deciduous and flowering trees and shrubs, was a circular drive, part of it for the public with the remainder reserved for patients. Other mixed plantings of trees and shrubs, arranged in the picturesque manner, created interest by framing vistas, emphasizing direction, or featuring a focal point.

Large expanses of open lawn were left in the center of the site, but specimen trees strategically placed enhanced these. Some of these original trees remain to this day, such as the Sweet Gum *(Liquidambar styraciflua),* a Connecticut State Champion; a Ginkgo *(Ginkgo biloba),* a New England Champion; and another Connecticut State champion, the Honey Locust *(Gleditsia triacanthos).* Another huge specimen, the Pecan *(Carya illinoensis),* is believed to have existed even before the Olmsted and Vaux plan. Edward D. Richardson, a prominent member of the Notable Tree Committee of the Connecticut Botanical Society, recently stated that "within this relatively small space is perhaps the greatest concentration of historic trees in Connecticut." It is this Committee that designates champion trees, those which are the oldest and largest in a state or region.

Near the Central Building, a large, circular flower garden with a conservatory in the center was planned, clearly a place where patients could enjoy a variety of flowers, both tropical and temperate, by strolling about or by sitting in the garden on benches provided along the paths. Taking off from this large garden was a tear-shaped circular walk that focused upon a building designed by Calvert Vaux called the Museum. Inside was a large pool table, and the walls were hung with engravings. Musical instruments, books, and other pictures also enhanced the room "for the amelioration of conditions of the unfortunate inmates."

The plan that Olmsted and Vaux drew was strong in concept, but many of the details for implementation were lacking. This was probably because shortly after its presentation, Olmsted took a leave of absence from his landscape work on Central Park in New York to become executive secretary of the United States Sanitary Commission during the Civil War. Fortunately for him and for Dr. Butler and his staff at the Retreat, Jacob Weidenmann had just been hired to come to Hartford as superintendent for the City Park, and he was asked to execute the Olmsted and Vaux plan.

The first step was to drain the wetland in the center of Retreat Park. This phase was not a problem for Weidenmann, since he was highly trained in these skills, and Olmsted and Vaux had already had Mr. George E. Waring, Jr., a civil engineer, draw plans for some of this drainage system. Work proceeded apace because volunteers raised substantial funds, so progress did not have to be gauged to budgetary restraints. Almost 10,000 feet of drainage tile were laid, and numerous brick sinks and surface drains were installed.

As part of the grading work, 4,500 cubic yards of soil were removed from the bank along Maple Avenue, the road, and walk beds, in order to establish proper grades and a subsurface. Trap stone was brought in as a base for these roads and paths, and the whole was then surfaced with 585 cubic yards of gravel. The edges of the lawn areas along the walks and drives were sodded with 4,800 square feet of turf, and the interior portions of eighteen acres were seeded to lawn. All this work was completed from June to November in 1862 at a cost of $6,036.00 (over $138,000 today).

Retreat Park was officially opened in 1863, and in his annual report for the previous year, Dr. Butler said: "Your Committee . . . thinks it due to Mr. Weidenmann, to express their entire satisfaction with the good taste and sound judgment he has shown in carrying out the plans, and with the efficiency and shrewdness of his general management. The results are greatly to his credit."

Evidently, the park was planted over a period of years because subsequently the Committee on Improvements at the Retreat thanks Weidenmann again in 1863, 1864, and 1865 for planting plans for shrubbery and also for the extension of the walk system. In the 1864 Annual Report, Dr. Butler states that the Retreat "continues to be under occasional obligations to the excellent taste and valuable suggestions of Mr. Weidenmann."

It attests to Weidenmann's energy, patience, and expertise that he

Olmsted and Vaux 1861 plan for the Retreat for the Insane
(The Institute of Living). From *Beautifying Country Homes*.

was able to perform these tasks while also getting started on implementing the plans for Bushnell Park, not an easy task because, as mentioned previously, certain of the Court of Common Council members were not totally convinced of the need for the Park, often impeding progress when the budget was approved incrementally. Weidenmann had not only to please these gentlemen, but also gauge the mammoth task of building the Park on the limited budget.

Much of Retreat Park exists today just as Olmsted and Vaux designed it. The inevitable parking lots have infringed along its edges, but Retreat Park still retains a similar main entrance on Retreat Avenue, the flowing circular walk around the perimeter, with cross walks between. Vaux's Museum Building also stands. As intended by Dr. John S. Butler in 1863, visitors are still welcome to use the park, as are the patients at the Institute.

Art Teacher
American School for the Deaf

One recent August day, when Connecticut was experiencing very hot and humid weather often referred to as "Dog Days," Gary E. Wait, current archivist at the American School for the Deaf in West Hartford, let his attention stray to an odd table in the corner stacked high with boxes of material to be catalogued and filed. His curiosity overcame him, and, in spite of the weather, he moved all of the boxes off the table and examined it carefully.

The table was old, obviously from the nineteenth century, because it had an ornate cast-iron base that would raise and lower, and also tilt back and forth. The square top of wood had a ridge up one side, but the ridge appeared to be one of those they used to put on drafting tables to keep pencils from rolling off. But why did it run up the side instead of along the bottom edge?

Wait inverted the table and saw evidence of empty screw holes, which suggested that the wood top had been shifted. He unscrewed it and found that originally the top had been attached with the ridge at the bottom of the board, not up one side. Why it had been changed, no one knows.

This prompted Wait to do some research into why a drafting or art table would have existed at the School in the nineteenth century. Much to his excitement, he discovered that classes in art were taught there, and that the instructor in 1861 was Jacob Weidenmann.

Proof of this was a bill submitted by Weidenmann to William W. Turner, the treasurer, for services as "drawing master." The bill not only paid Weidenmann's salary of $100.00 for the year, but it also charged for portfolios, paper, sepia color, frames, water color brushes, and related items.

Little else is known of Weidenmann's classes at the School. One wonders how he had the strength and energy to conduct his work developing the City Park, implementing the plans at the Retreat, and still find time to teach art classes, probably in the evening, at the American School for the Deaf, all during his first year in Hartford.

After this series of classes was completed, Weidenmann did not plan to offer others. A group of young men in the community pleaded with him to offer a class in practical drawing covering a variety of subjects, but Weidenmann did not have time to devote to such a course. However, being the strong believer in education that he was, he agreed to organize a series of courses for the young men, and to enlist the assistance of some of his fellow artists as teachers. First, he organized a group of prominent citizens to fund and administer the series so that the students would receive the classes free of charge. His friend and former client, James Howard, along with James G. Batterson, and Samuel Colt, were but three of the benefactors. Classes were offered every evening from seven to nine, except Sunday, and the teachers were: Weidenmann for perspective, freehand, and geometric drawing on Monday and Friday; architectural drawing with George Keller on Tuesday; Martin Insbach taught machine drawing on Wednesday and Saturday, and M. Conrad taught monument and sculptural drawing on Thursday.

The City of Hartford Lithograph

In 1864, Jacob Weidenmann tried another moneymaking venture, and that was to publish a splendid birds-eye view lithograph of the City of Hartford. How this came about remains a mystery. To be sure, Weidenmann was a skilled artist in his own right, but he was not a lithographer, though he probably had an interest in that art, especially as it portrayed landscapes. This lithograph in particular may have caught his eye because it has as its focal point Weidenmann's emerging creation, the new City Park. It is not known if he had an influence on the lithographer's choice of vantage point, which features the Park, or if he became interested in the lithograph after it had been completed.

The landscape draftsman and lithographer who created this birds-eye view of Hartford was John Bachmann, considered then as now the finest lithographer of the mid-19th Century. Very little is known of his life, other than that he probably was born and studied in Germany and then came to the United States in about 1848. Between 1849 and 1884, Bachmann created fifty-three city views; thirty-three of them were various aspects of New York. He also did two of Boston, and seven of New Orleans. He had worked throughout the south and as far west as Superior, Wisconsin. Bachmann traveled about with his work, and he is known to have lived in New York, as well as Hoboken, New Jersey, where he made two views of the city, finally settling in New Orleans where he died in 1884.

His birds-eye views were acclaimed because of their high level perspectives, so chosen to show street patterns and other details, as well as architectural facades of buildings. Choosing high vantage points also enabled him to show an entire city, or at least most of it. He was noted, as were other lithographers, for showing uncompleted projects as completed. When he made the Hartford view, for example, Bushnell Park was not yet finished, but it is shown completed, and in his 1862 view of Washington, he shows the Washington monument, then in construction, as completed.

The view of Hartford, printed by F. Heppenheimer of New York, focuses on the City Park in the center, with a beam of light shining on and around it to attract the eye. In the foreground is the Park River with the railroad tracks paralleling it. Typical of Bachmann's work, as a way of giving life to the scene, a train is shown puffing its way from the station, and people are visible crossing the bridge across the Park River. Hartford's street pattern is quite clear, and along Main Street, one can see all of the church spires, the State House, and the Atheneum. To the right of the new Park are residential streets, where now the State Office Buildings stand, and on the site of the present State Capitol is Trinity College adjacent to the Park. In the far distance is the Connecticut River with its busy port and hills in the background.

Bachmann was noted for his modern approach, abandoning old concepts. In the case of the Hartford view, he features the new and modern form of transportation and shipping, the railroad, and the new concept of public parks, rather than the traditional seaport and main street approach most commonly portrayed by artists who had preceded him as well as those who were his contemporaries.

The extent to which publication of this view of the City of Hartford enriched Jacob Weidenmann, or how and for how long it was sold, is not known.

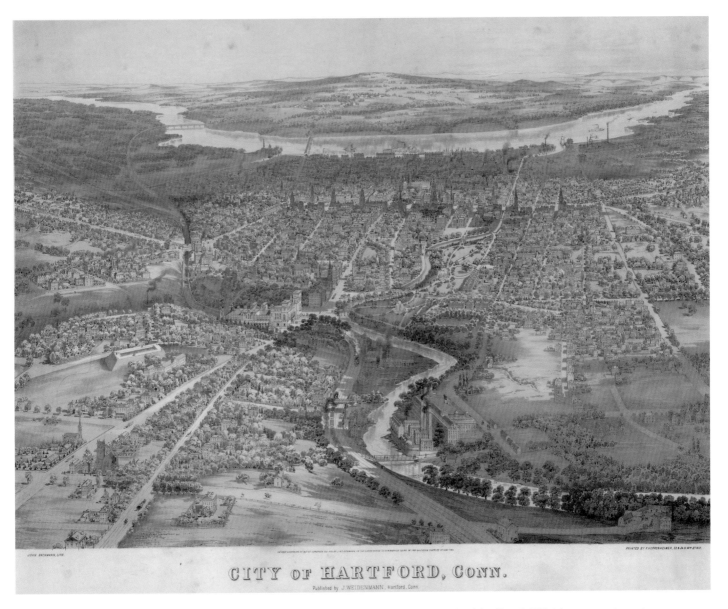

CITY OF HARTFORD, CONN.

Published by J. WEIDENMANN, Hartford, Conn.

The Hartford lithograph, published by Jacob Weidenmann in 1864. The City Park is in the center. Factory, lower center, is the Sharpe Rifle Factory, later Pope Manufacturing. Large building left of center, with towers, is the original railroad station.

Butler Homestead
(Now the Butler-McCook Homestead)

In 1865, Miss Mary Sheldon (1816–1887) engaged Jacob Weidenmann to draw plans to make over her existing gardens, which stood within an acre of ground behind and to one side of the old Butler Homestead built in 1782. Miss Sheldon had moved into the Butler Homestead on Main Street in 1837 because her father had died sometime before, and during that year her mother, Eliza Royce Sheldon (1797–1858), married her deceased husband's cousin, John Butler (1780–1847). In 1840, a daughter, Eliza Sheldon Butler, was born to them.

John Butler, the son of Daniel (1751–1812), descended from Richard Butler, one of Hartford's original settlers in 1636. He was a distant cousin of Dr. John S. Butler, superintendent of the Retreat, mentioned above.

In 1856, when Eliza Sheldon Butler turned sixteen, her mother took her and her stepsister, Mary Sheldon, on the Grand Tour of Europe, making Paris their base. They spent two-and-one-half years abroad, and during that time there were periods of schooling in French, art, and music for the young Eliza. They visited many American friends who were also touring abroad. They also had the opportunity to observe gardens and gardening, and both Mary and Eliza became interested in the subject.

Sadly, Mrs. Butler died near the end of their journey, so the sisters then went on to stay with friends in England during their period of mourning. We can presume that they also visited gardens while there, which further spurred their interest in the subject. In 1859, the sisters returned to Hartford and the old homestead.

We have no indication what the gardens were like at the time Mr. Weidenmann was engaged to draw plans for a fee of six hundred dollars, as much as he was making as Hartford's Superintendent of the Park (Bushnell). We do know that there was a large vegetable garden, with a long central path to the rear, or east, of the homestead, which stood at the very front of the one-acre lot on Main Street. Also, the records show that a pit house and cold frames had been built in 1850 along the north boundary of the lot. During their grand tour, the Louis Weld family, cousins of Mrs. Butler, occupied the house. Their son, Mason, publisher and co-editor of *The Homestead, A Weekly Magazine of Agriculture*

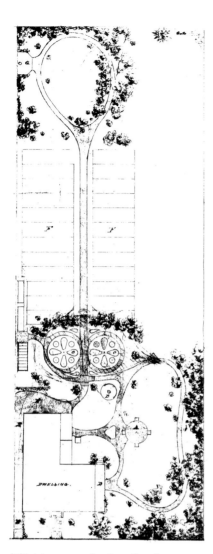

Weidenmann's plan for the
Butler Homestead gardens.

and Horticulture, used the gardens and grounds to experiment with various new plants. When Mary and Eliza returned from their grand tour, they installed running water in the homestead and removed the woodshed and outhouse from the garden.

Though the sisters were very well read in the field of gardening and design, they obviously did not feel competent to re-design their own garden. Nonetheless, letters and documents in the family archives indicate that they had certain wishes which Weidenmann was asked to incorporate into the final plan. They wanted the old family vegetable garden right where it had been, in the middle of the lot, rather than at the far end, where Weidenmann usually placed them. Mary and Eliza also wanted a flower garden and lawn, accented by picturesque shrub groupings, just like those they read about in books by Downing and Loudon, which they had in their library.

Weidenmann, as he usually did, utilized the natural merits of the site to enhance the plan. The house, sited at street level, and the terrace behind it, were about six feet above the level of the vegetable garden, separated from it by a gradual slope. He used this feature to advantage. First he removed the stepping stones leading to and through the vegetable garden and made a paved terrace outside the kitchen door for viewing the gardens below, and possibly for use as a work place. Then, by some regrading, he placed the flower parterres at the base of the slope near the vegetable gardens, a good site because parterre patterns show best when viewed from above. All of the walks between the parterre sections, as well as the central one in the vegetable garden, were surfaced with fine gravel, a popular treatment at that time, but the vegetable garden's central walk was bordered with turf for accent, and to also make it more ornamental as a connecting path between the two natural-style gardens.

The major natural garden was south of the homestead in an area where Weidenmann had to install extensive drainage pipes as well as service for the central fountain. The main path to this garden came from the house and the new veranda, designed by Weidenmann, directly south to meet the walk that circled the perimeter of this space. Where these walks joined, a ten-foot diameter pool with a central fountain jet was built of Portland (Connecticut) brownstone. At four evenly spaced intervals within the curbing were raised platforms supporting ornamental pots of flowers. The outer edges of this natural space, between the curved walk and the boundary fences, were planted heavily with shrubs. In the center, surrounding the pool, was an open lawn.

Unfortunately, the planting plans are not extant; however, in the late 1950s, Eliza's daughter, Frances McCook recalled that several plants that grew in the garden, namely a bald cypress, a laburnum, a fringe tree, and perhaps the horse chestnut, were some of the originals planted.

It was the walk system that tied the various parts of this garden together. Weidenmann designed a branch that left the circular walk of the natural garden around the parterre gardens. It then ran down the center of the vegetable gardens to the rear of the property, and there he formed it into an oval, which surrounded an open lawn containing some accent shrub plantings. Again, the perimeter of this space, between the walk and the boundaries, was heavily planted with shrubs. The main feature of this garden was a rustic pavilion at one side, where visitors could sit and passively enjoy the landscape.

As a transition piece between the front natural garden and the parterres, Weidenmann designed another rustic structure, which he called a "rustic seat," rather than a pavilion, because of its smaller size. Rustic seats, built of logs and twigs, were popular during this era, and this one was perfectly placed for viewing both the parterres and the natural garden.

The garden was completed on May 31, 1865, except for some trees that had to await fall planting. The following year, Eliza Butler married John James McCook (1843–1927) a relative through his mother, who was a Sheldon. McCook was ordained as rector of St. John's Church in East Hartford in 1866, and in 1883 he was appointed professor of modern languages at Trinity College, his alma mater. McCook held these two positions for most of the rest of his life, and in addition conducted studies on social reform, having become interested in the plight of the homeless in the Hartford area.

The original Butler-McCook garden remains in part. The second natural garden at the end of the long garden path is no longer there, but the one nearer the house is extant, complete with its pool. Most of Weidenmann's veranda was modified when the McCook's son added his medical office to that side of the homestead. The parterres have been slightly revised, but the general pattern is still evident, and the stone terrace above remains, as does the ancient pit greenhouse. The rustic pavilion and seat no longer stand. On April 5, 2005, the author visited this garden, just as the lawn was turning green. The exact position of the vegetable garden was evident due to a richer hue of the green grass from years of added organic matter.

Edmund Grant Howe was born on Spring Hill in Mansfield, Connecticut, in 1807. Like many young men of that era, he left the hard work of the farm in favor of an easier life in the city. Eventually he became a prominent dry goods merchant and banker in Hartford, where he settled in 1829. He also was the first president of the Hartford-Wethersfield Horse Railway Company. By the mid-1860s, he owned the largest estate on "Millionaire Row," the name applied locally to a section of Hartford Avenue along Wethersfield Cove. Howe's mansion was at 390 Hartford Avenue, and was served by his Horse Railway.

The owner of the Brown-Thomson Company in Hartford, a well-known department store, built this large, square, mansard-roofed mansion, with a wrap-around veranda on the south and southeast sides, in 1850. Mr. Brown sold it to Howe in the early 1860s, and soon Jacob Weidenmann was engaged to improve the grounds, which swept from the high ground, surrounding the mansion close to Hartford Avenue, all the way to Wethersfield Cove. Howe's estate is now gone because the land was subdivided in the late nineteenth century into seven building lots, and the house was destroyed.

No plans for this project are extant, nor are there any detailed descriptions of the grounds, but they are presumed to have been executed in the natural style like most of Weidenmann's projects. In *Beautifying Country Homes*, which he was soon to publish, Weidenmann included a sketch of a rustic pavilion that he had designed for this landscape. It was situated at the edge of the Cove along a meandering walk, shaded by an elm. The pavilion sat high on an eight to ten foot log base, perhaps for better viewing, but also because the Cove tends to overflow its banks during rainy seasons. The stair and pavilion balustrade were made of natural tree branches, while the shelter itself had a distinct Oriental and bracketed roof. This eclectic combination of the log construction with the Oriental style was common during the Victorian era.

The text that accompanies the sketch of this pavilion states that "a rustic summer house, on elevated ground, or near a bank of a lake, is highly ornamental, but before copying the clumsy illustrations given in most all books on landscape gardening, we would appeal to the good taste of the improver to see that proportion is combined with neatness."

The Edmund G. Howe pavilion, Wethersfield, Connecticut.
From *Beautifying Country Homes*.

James Leland Howard (1818–1906), and his wife, Anna Gilbert Howard, built their house just three blocks north of Farmington Avenue, at 67 Collins Street, in 1861. It was a large two story Italian villa, with a tower of four stories. Atop the main house was a cupola-belvedere.

Mr. Howard was born in Windsor, Vermont and at the age of fifteen went to New York and entered the mercantile business. Five years later, in 1838, he moved to Hartford and entered the firm of Hurlburt and Howard, manufacturers of carriage and saddle hardware. As railroads expanded, Hurlburt and Howard added the manufacture of furnishings for railroad cars. Howard soon bought out his partner, and the firm name was changed to James L. Howard and Company, situated at 176–178 Asylum Avenue.

In addition to his successful business career, James L. Howard served on the original Board of Park Commissioners for the city of Hartford, serving as its chairman in 1870 when Weidenmann published, *Beautifying Country Homes*. The book was "respectfully and affectionately dedicated" to him. In 1887, Howard was elected Lieutenant Governor of the State of Connecticut for one term, to serve with Governor Phineas C. Lounsbury.

The Howards hired Jacob Weidenmann to design a landscape for their new home grounds. The site was small, consisting of one acre, with some complicated problems to solve. Extensive grading was required on site in order to meet the owners' program of needs, and, to use Weidenmann's own words "scarcely a foot of ground [remained] in its original position. Although but fifteen feet from the street, the greatest difficulty was found in obtaining proper access to the side entrance door and service entrance facing the street. The general formation of the land required the house to stand eight feet above street grade . . . . A tasteful arrangement of stone steps and handsome copings lead from the elevated [street sidewalk] . . . to the main entrance of the house." Another walk from the street sidewalk led to the cellar door, requiring no steps, and a walk branched from it around the rear of the house to the kitchen door.

Having solved these access and grade problems and thereby providing convenient pedestrian entrances and service deliveries, the next problem was to provide access to the main front door and the veranda door, by horse and carriage. Weidenmann achieved this

The Howard residence several years after the landscape was installed.

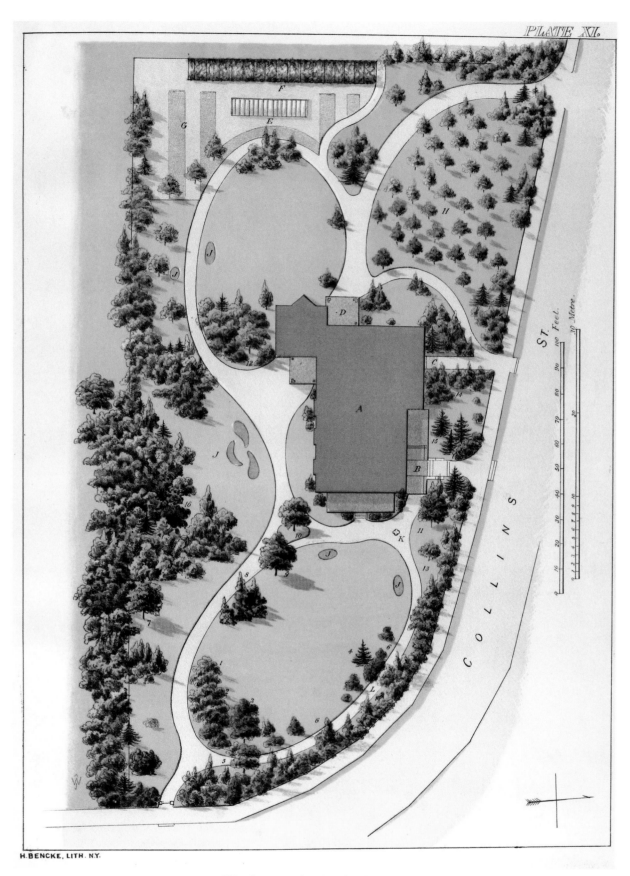

PLATE XI.

H. BENCKE, LITH. N.Y.

Weidenmann's plan for the Howard Residence,
Collins Street, Hartford. From *Beautifying Country Homes*.

by designing a direct but curved drive to these entrances, with ample space for carriages to turn around at the front door. Off this pleasant drive he created two roundabout loops, or walks, one encircling the front yard, and the other surrounding a more private pleasure ground. At the very rear, or west end of the property, a service drive was planned passing through the vegetable garden area and around the orchard to reach the kitchen entrance. Along the pleasure drives, at intervals close to the house, were flower beds, some circular and others formed as tear drops.

In Weidenmann's usual manner, the perimeter of the property was heavily planted with a variety of plant species of various forms and textures. In comparing this plan to some of his other residential work, however, these plantings seem thicker and heavier, no doubt because both the north and east sides of this property were exposed to the street, and the remaining boundaries were close to neighboring properties. The objective to create an ambiance of park-like privacy was achieved.

Within these grounds, specimen trees such as Norway spruce, sweet gum, horse chestnut, magnolias, various maples, European beech, and flowering cherries were carefully planted as accents or focal points, and, particularly, to frame internal vistas. Along the entrance drive, trees and groupings of shrubs were placed so that only glimpses of the residence would be seen while driving towards it in a carriage, and then the entire house would unfold visually upon arrival. Also, Weidenmann used trees and shrubs to define the two major pleasure lawns in order to create intimate outdoor "rooms." Unfortunately this landscape is no longer extant.

The Suburban Villa of Timothy Stanley
New Britain, Connecticut

Jacob Weidenmann's practice as a landscape architect (the title he was now using) was expanding outside the Hartford area. At some point in the late 1860s he designed the grounds for an extensive estate in the growing city of New Britain. His client Timothy Wadsworth Stanley (1817–1897), was considered the wealthiest man in New Britain. Mr. Stanley, along with his three brothers, had founded the Stanley Rule and Level Manufacturing Company, which sometime after his death became a part of the Stanley Works, founded by another branch of his family, for the manufacture of carpentry and other tools. Timothy Stanley was also active in banking circles, and for several years served as president of the Savings Bank of New Britain.

Stanley owned a four-acre site sloping east with expansive views overlooking the town of New Britain and the valley beyond. In order to site his gothic revival mansion on level ground, considerable grading was required, resulting in extensive terracing behind the house to accommodate the grade changes. A long four-foot wide walk led in a curving sweep along terraces, through an orchard, a large symmetrically laid out vegetable garden, and on to a pavilion, situated on still higher ground for viewing the valley below. On the lowest part of the site, Weidenmann placed the barn and stables, though he reserved the furthest corner, probably at the owner's request, for a separate building lot, perhaps for the estate manager.

A wide entrance drive encircled the mansion, serving both the front and rear doors, and then it continued on to the barn and stable area. Branching from the drive was a walk to the barn, laid out in a characteristic curve which, along with the curving drive, formed an ornamentally planted roundabout. Weidenmann was a master at articulating curves in the landscape, taking great care to make them flow organically, gently with the natural terrain, and devoid of sharp turns or instant reverses.

He designed the plantings for this estate in his usual way, heavily planting the perimeter of the property, and then strategically placing picturesque grouping of trees to frame vistas, to emphasize the ground plan, or as focal pieces within the central grounds. Of particular note in this plan is his use of distinct forms, such as Lombardy poplars, and pointed evergreens, probably to dramatize the hilliness of the site. His usual interplay of textures also prevails, especially as focal points for the created vistas.

It is interesting to note that the Stanley estate was adjacent to the parcel of land of thirty-six acres, situated further up the slope, that the city of New Britain purchased in 1856 to build a reservoir. Eleven years later, Timothy Stanley's fourth cousin, Frederick T. Stanley (1802–1893), wrote to Frederick Law Olmsted inviting him to come to New Britain to consult on the site for a period of two days. This site, named Walnut Hill Park, is still in use today. Mr. Timothy Stanley's mansion stands nearby, but the grounds have been sub-divided.

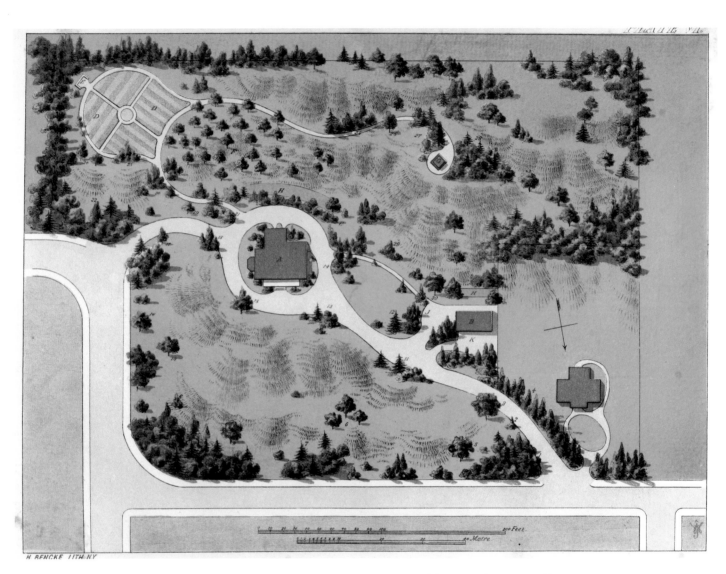

Weidenmann's plan for the Timothy Stanley Villa.
From *Beautifying Country Homes*.

Facing page: Weidenmann's plans for the Charles E. Brainard grapery
and entrance gate. From *American Garden Architecture*.

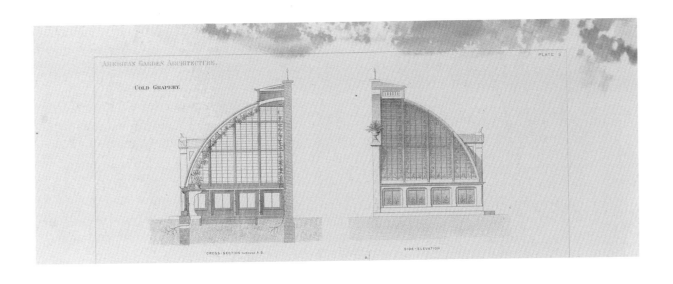

COLD GRAPERY.

CROSS-SECTION through A.B.

SIDE-ELEVATION

ELEVATION.

PLAN.

On Capitol Avenue, in Hartford, were several mansions where the expansive parking lots east of the State Office Buildings are now. One of these, at 119 Capitol Avenue, was the home of Charles E. Brainard (1813–1889) and his wife, Mary J. Goodwin, daughter of Major James Goodwin. Brainard was active in the metal importing business started by his father. At the time of his death Charles Brainard was president of State Bank. He owned extensive real estate on Capitol Avenue, and all of the property on the south side of Mulberry Street, save for one lot. He also owned much real estate on Main Street between the Wadsworth Atheneum and St. John's Church.

It is not known if Weidenmann designed the entire landscape for Brainard's large brownstone house; we have only the plan for the grapery and the entrance gate. These designs show Weidenmann's architectural skills in their well-proportioned and delicate, yet functional, design.

Graperies were popular in the mid-nineteenth century as a place to grow grapes for winter use. Samuel Colt built the largest one in the state, or perhaps the world, at Armsmear, his Hartford estate not far away from Capitol Avenue. Brainard's grapery was referred to as a "cold grapery," meaning that the temperature was kept cool, at about 50–55 degrees, suitable for the culture of grapes. Often graperies were built as lean-to structures against a high masonry wall which acted as a solar collector. For Brainard, however, Weidenmann designed a free-standing structure with a domed top which sat upon a brick foundation coped with Portland brownstone to match the details of the mansion. As the glass sides of the grapery converged at the top, they were capped with a four-hipped roof with an ornamental cast-iron rail around its edge. The glass sashes were constructed of yellow pine. Jacob Weidenmann charged Brainard $850.00 for these plans, which included supervising the work (about $11,000.00 today).

The front of the property was enclosed by a curb wall topped with a balustrade, probably of brownstone to conform to the walls of the mansion. The gate that Weidenmann designed swung open as most gates do, but in the process, it could be folded. This beautiful, delicately designed gate, with flowing, organic curves, artistically incorporated Charles Brainard's initials below an elaborate central finial. The gates hung on two columns which clearly and strongly defined the property's entrance.

New Britain Avenue Subdivision
Hartford, Connecticut

Jacob Weidenmann had a bad habit of not dating most of his plans
so we do not know exactly when he drew the "Map of Valuable
Building Lots" for E.L. Cleveland and William G. Allen. The plan,
drawn to a scale of forty feet to the inch, was for twenty-seven
house lots off of New Britain Avenue in Hartford, just a block away
from the Retreat, or The Institute of Living as it is now called. Lots
one through twelve faced on Webster Street and the remainder
were planned on either side of Ellsworth Street, both of these streets
running south and perpendicular to New Britain Avenue.

This was not a residential subdivision like Llewellyn Park, or Hill
Park, which Weidenmann had worked on before; instead, it was
what we would refer to today as a "cookie-cutter" project, each lot a
minimum width and depth in order to cram as many as possible
onto the site. The plan shows no provision for street tree planting
or any other landscape amenities.

It is obvious that Weidenmann took on this commission following
the wishes of his clients to extract as many building lots as possible
from the site. He does include the following statement on the
plan: "This property embraces nearly seven acres, and commands
one of the finest views of the Connecticut River Valley of any locality
in the State." The plan is signed "drawn by Jacob Weidenman,
surveyor." E.B. and C. Kellogg, Hartford, Connecticut printed it for
distribution.

Apparently, these lots sold quickly, and today one can see houses
from the mid-nineteenth century still standing.

"Beautifying Country Homes"

The year 1868 was memorable for the Weidenmanns. Their third daughter and last child, Marguerite, was born at their residence on 88 Church Street. It was also the year that Jacob began gathering material for a book on residential landscape gardening. It was a good time for him to do this because the City Park was virtually completed, and though he had the additional responsibilities of maintaining and refurbishing South Green and the State House grounds, as well as superintending Cedar Hill Cemetery, his workload was somewhat lighter.

As we have seen, Weidenmann was always looking for ways to earn extra money. He obviously had a talent for organization and for clearly stating his ideas and concepts not only in plan view but also in writing. This talent gave him the confidence to write a book, using his growing file of plans and specifications for both his public and private commissions as its basis. His goal was to produce a practical, easy-to-use book on landscape gardening for private residences.

The country was becoming more industrialized each year with an average of five percent of the population per decade, since 1790, leaving rural agricultural pursuits and entering business and industry. In 1790, over ninety percent of the population had been engaged in some aspect of agriculture, while by 1868 the figure had dropped to fifty-three percent. As the countryside built-up, a movement was begun to construct suburban dwellings in settings that approximated the natural landscape of the rural countryside.

Andrew Jackson Downing had advocated this approach in his *Treatise on the Theory and Practice of Landscape Gardening*, first published in 1849. Several other authors followed Downing's model and published their own books in a similar format, such as, G. M. Kern, who wrote *Practical Landscape Gardening* and had it printed in Cincinnati, Ohio, in 1855. Ten years after this, Robert Morris Copeland's *Country Life: A Handbook of Agriculture, Horticulture, and Landscape Gardening* appeared. Articles were printed in journals such as the *Horticulturist,* all promoting park-like settings for suburban dwellings. The very year that Weidenmann published his *Beautifying Country Homes*, in 1870, Frank J. Scott came out with his book called *The Art of Beautifying Suburban Home Grounds*. The modernization of printing at this time facilitated the production of books that could be sold at reasonable prices.

Weidenmann's book, however, was different from all of these long and lengthy works, ranging from Kern's 328 page opus to Copeland's 912 page tome. Instead his was divided into two parts, the first part of forty pages held text on how to landscape suburban grounds. The second part was devoted to twenty-four plans of various places, with a descriptive page for each plan that pointed out the particular challenges for the designer, as well as a description of the plan itself, and in most cases, the plants used. In his prefacing remarks, Weidenmann states that it was his goal to "briefly and practically" present methods for improving the "suburban home effectively and with economy." He then goes on to say that he will present solutions to common problems, not unique ones, and that in the interest of being brief he will not give detailed rationales for the solutions. In today's jargon, he was writing a practical "how-to" book, one of the first of its kind in the field of landscape architecture.

Beautifying Country Homes is exceedingly well written. It is well organized, clear, and forthright in its approach. It is amazing that Weidenmann, a recent immigrant, had such a good command of the English language. One could easily assume that a good editor was by his side, but a review of his other writings, such as the descriptions that he wrote to accompany plans that he drew for clients, or his correspondence, reveal that he had mastered the language. He wrote in a manner free of the paragraph-long sentences that were the signature of so many nineteenth century authors. Here is an example of his clear and inspiring writing:

> All cannot enjoy the privilege of a stroll in the King of Parks — the central Park of New York. Comparatively few can view its extended lawns, or its bold cliffs and caves, admire its triumphs of architectural taste, or note how the skillful artist has converted a vast plain into hills and dales, and varied it with lakes and cascades, shady founts, and open lawns. But all can make their country homes attractive and lovely, and enjoy the beauties of nature about their house and fireside.

In his preface, Weidenmann states that his objective is to lead the reader through the various phases of landscaping the country, or suburban house: siting the house, draining and grading the ground, designing and constructing drives and walks, seeding the ground, planting trees and shrubs, and finally, estimating costs for all of the work.

In the second part of the book, Weidenmann uses the case study approach for giving examples of how to apply the principles set forth in Part One. Today, landscape architects use the case study approach freely to illustrate points they wish to make both in written or spoken works. Weidenmann's presentation is the first known example of this approach as we know it today. Eight of the plans that he uses as case studies are his own; one other for which an author is not identified may also be his. Five other case study plans are those of his close friends: Eugene Baumann, Ignatz Pilat, Frederick Law Olmsted and Calvert Vaux. The remaining plans are by seven other professionals.

Weidenmann, it seems, had several objectives in mind in selecting the plans he used. First of all, he wished to promote his own works, and he carefully selected his plans to show that he had worked not only in the New York and Hartford areas, but also in Cincinnati and elsewhere. All of the plans he used are for projects that were designed anew, no makeovers, such as the garden that he designed for Miss Sheldon at the Butler-McCook House. While this was an excellent design, it has too much of the influence of the owner, as well as of the previous garden plan.

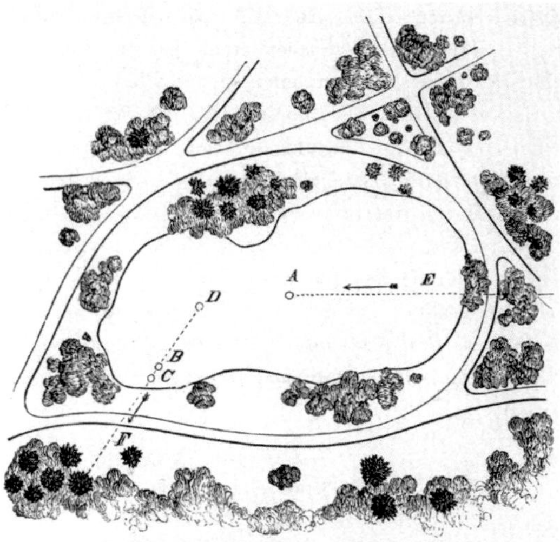

Within the text of Part One are over eighty illustrations. Most of these are details taken from Weidenmann's own plans, such as plans and cross-sections for his drainage and roadwork in the City Park and at Cedar Hill Cemetery, or planting designs or garden pavilions from his various other projects. Weidenmann was employing his usual resourcefulness by pulling together his various sketches and plans, filling in any obvious gaps with those of his landscape architect colleagues, and producing a very useful book on the various phases of landscaping a country house.

Fig. 56.—CITY PARK POND, HARTFORD, CONN.

Pond details drawn by Weidenmann. From *Beautifying Country Homes*.

The book begins with a discussion on how to site a house on the grounds. Weidenmann advises his readers to set the house back from the street for a park-like setting, and placing it to one side on a lot so that the park can flow to the rear of the site without being interrupted. He recommends laying out drives and walks in "easy curves," never in straight lines or in serpentine patterns, always remembering, however, that curves should not be such that they "create a desire to shorten the distance between the two objects by making a track through the lawns." In other words, it is all right to curve, but always remember that the shortest distance between two points is a straight line, so don't curve too much. We have stated previously that Weidenmann was a master at laying out free-flowing curves for walks and drives. His designs were highly artistic in their gracefulness, yet they met every functional requirement.

Part of creating the natural, rural setting for the suburban house was the inclusion of an expansive lawn. Weidenmann states that the lawn is "the basis of the whole ornamental pleasure ground," thus creating a vast carpet for the entire grounds. Preferably, the grounds should have "swells" for interest, but no hollows where water may collect. In other words, undulations create interest. He considers the lawn so important a setting and unifying element for the grounds that he stated that they should be planted "sparingly" with no shrubs and trees immediately around the residence in order to allow extensive views, and that thick planting should only be employed around the perimeter of the property and to screen neighbors.

Weidenmann presents an extensive discussion on what grass seed to use and on the care of the lawn. The lawn seed mixtures are quite different from the refined types we use today. Even the mixture he presents as "fine" contains white clover, rough stalked meadow grass, and perennial rye grass, all species we consider coarse today. He stresses the need for adequate fertilization, by allowing the clippings to fall and decay, in addition to adding peat moss, muck, wood ashes, plaster dust (probably as a form of limestone), ground bone meal, and Peruvian guano. Commercial preparations for both seed mixtures and fertilizer blends were not yet available.

The section on drainage is extensive considering the size of the book, but then, this was one of Weidenmann's specialties, and a place where he had many fine examples to present from his work at the Retreat, the City Park, and Cedar Hill Cemetery. Yet he says that he is just presenting the most common of problems, and for more detail one should consider referring to the book, *Draining for Profit*, written by Colonel George E. Waring, Jr., with whom he had worked on the drainage for the City Park and the Retreat.

Weidenmann then presents numerous cross-section sketches on laying the beds of roads, showing five different layers, from coarse to fine, and emphasizing the importance of rolling extensively at each layer. He then repeats the same information, but reduced in scale, for the laying of walks. Discussions follow on planning walks and even on creating rambles, such as the one that he and Baumann designed for Llewellyn Park. He then describes how to decide on the widths of walks, ranging from three to ten feet, depending on their use.

In his section on grading the ground surface, Weidenmann writes that the process is often overdone. "Do not touch nature's gentle rise and fall," he says, however "imperfect dents" should be repaired. He advises that embankments should be avoided, if possible, and that any change in grade should be gentle, not sudden.

Weidenmann obviously felt the same about fences and walls for residences as he did for cemeteries; they should be avoided because they interrupt the flow of the eye across the park-like landscape. He does concede that they may be necessary for certain purposes, and goes on to discuss the pros and cons of wood, cast iron, and wire fences, suggesting that the latter is less obtrusive. He is definitely opposed to picket fences, not only because they are expensive to build and care for, but also because they are "repulsive, stiff, and unnatural." Hedges, he advises, should only be used for screening, such as for service yards.

Having discussed the ground plan, Weidenmann then writes extensively about planting design, one of the three-dimensional aspects of the plan. A quarter of the text in Part One is devoted to plants and planting. He discusses the principles to be employed in designing plantings: the designer should consider plant form, branching, color, and texture of the trunks of trees for their year round effect. He should consider the seasonal effect of flowers and leaves; evergreens should be employed for their form and for their winter effect; soil conditions should be considered for each plant species. He then treats the design of the plantings themselves, stressing groupings for lawns, for the rear of the property, or spatial definition, to define roads and walks, or to provide background for garden features such as benches or seats. He advocates masses to conceal fence lines.

Weidenmann, unlike many garden writers of his period, is not an advocate of extensive flower gardens without reason. He stresses the importance of planning them according to the time available for their maintenance. He further advocates their placement close to houses, or walks, so that they may be seen and enjoyed. It is interesting to note in Part Two of the book that his own plans use flower gardens sparingly, and not in highly geometric forms, though he does present some of these forms in Part One, as examples.

As mentioned earlier, Weidenmann advises that "a landscape without water is imperfect, no matter how beautiful otherwise it may be." For his discussion on this subject, he uses several sketches of his work at Cedar Hill Cemetery, and he further shows, through sketches and cross-sections, systems for creating water cascades, or for installing fountains.

There is a brief section in the text on the use of garden ornaments — sundials, pavilions, kiosks, rustic seats, statues, and vases (urns). In both this section, as well as in the planting design section, he shows and tells how best to incorporate these features into the plan, but he ends with a word of warning: do not "overload" the landscape. As we study Weidenmann's own plans in Part Two, we can observe the great restraint he employed in this regard.

After a section on garden tools, and another extensive one on estimating costs for landscape construction and installation, there is a section on front yards and city lots. Here he states that even in urban settings, extensive front yards should extend along the sides of the house. Front yards, he says, can be combined visually, "as to give a suburban-like appearance to a place, street, or even a single house."

To illustrate these points, he shows a sketch of the combined front yards of the George Beach and Charles Cheney residences, which once stood in Hartford, on Farmington Avenue where the Aetna Insurance Company campus is now. Beach, along with his brothers, was an importer of "dye stuffs" from the Caribbean, and in addition was president of the First National Bank of Hartford. He had a keen interest in landscape gardening and horticulture, and designed his own plan (Plate IV in the book). Beach served as a member of the Park Commission in Hartford, from 1860-1869, and as its president for the last three of those years.

It is not known who designed Charles Cheney's landscape, but it is believed that Weidenmann had a part in combining the entrance gate for the two properties, and in designing the plantings for the front lawns so they would appear as one broad sweep of parkland. A sketch for this scheme is pictured in the text of Weidenmann's book. Charles Cheney, along with his brothers, founded the Cheney Silk Manufacturing Company, which started first on Morgan Street in Hartford, but later moved to land near the old Cheney homestead on Hartford Road, in Manchester, Connecticut, where they built a new factory and homes.

The Cheney "compound" in Manchester, consisting of the residences of several relatives, carried out the concept of the common lawn. Here they made a vast greensward, the size of a public park, neatly embellished with some specimen trees. Most certainly Charles Cheney was impressed with the concept that Weidenmann had suggested for his and George Beach's properties in Hartford, so that he expanded upon it for the new Cheney houses in Manchester. Fortunately this fine example exists today.

The final section of Part One deals with the layout of cemeteries, basically advocating the open lawn plan discussed earlier in this work, under the Cedar Hill Cemetery section, Chapter Two, and greatly enlarged in a book that Weidenmann was to write twenty years later, entitled *Modern Cemeteries* (see Chapter Seven).

As we analyze Weidenmann's plans in Part Two of his book, we find that they illustrate the use of the lawns, drives, and walks

Sketch plan showing the integration of the Charles Cheney and George Beach lawns, Farmington Avenue, Hartford. From *Beautifying Country Homes*.

as unifying and integrating elements for his plans; these features are what hold the plan together. All three-dimensional features, such as the residence, stables, orchards, gardens, and pavilions, are artistically integrated into the ground plan rather than appearing as separate parts or additions to the plan. Even on rugged topography, such as that of the Stanley Villa, Plate VI, this artistic integration is achieved. As we study Weidenmann's plans in his book, such as Plates VI and XI, and compare these with Plate XII, we can easily appreciate his skill as an artist. The Plate XII plan reads as a third of the site for the residence, a third for the pleasure grounds, and a third for the barn and gardens. The walks and drives are stiffly executed, not organically articulated, and they are not used in a manner to integrate the various parts of the site.

Beautifying Country Homes, which presented each plan as a color lithograph, was a great critical success in its day. It was praised in the *Horticulturist*, and Olmsted thought it a good and basic "standard work," meaning that it would serve the reader well as a how-to, case study book. Several praised it as one of the best books published on the subject, including the art critic Marianna Griswold Van Rensselaer in her book *Landscape Gardening*. Unfortunately, because of the cost of the color lithographs, it did not have the broad distribution or multiple printings that it deserved, and the book, today, has become a rare collector's item.

About the time that the book was published by Orange Judd and Company in 1870, Weidenmann took leave from his responsibilities in Hartford, including his private practice. He spent a year in Switzerland visiting his mother. His father had died in 1864, and while his mother was faring well and was capable of managing her financial affairs successfully, she was anxious to see her son after fourteen years. She was proud of his success in America, and she was especially anxious to meet her three granddaughters.

It seems quite surprising that a young man, ascending to the pinnacle of his career, and with a growing family, would take an entire year's leave from his work. Was Weidenmann "burned out" from his intense work in building the Park and establishing Cedar Hill Cemetery, and executing all of his other varied commissions? Or was it just another one of his impulsive acts, such as when he purchased the family of slaves at auction in Peru? We can only speculate that he had accumulated a little cash from his extra commissions, foresaw some income from his book, and needed to visit his mother after fourteen years. He may have been tired from the stress of his work and decided to take a long sabbatical without considering the consequences.

PLATE II.

Weidenmann's
plan for city lots
showing integrated
front lawns.
From *Beautifying
Country Homes*.

New York: Olmsted Alliance

Jacob Weidenmann spent a long vacation in Switzerland, primarily to visit his mother. His daughter Marguerite, in some accounts, says that he stayed two years; in others, one year; and in still others more than a year. We know that he left after the publication of his book in 1870, and that he was back in the United States by late 1871. Knowing his inquisitive and restless nature, and his constant desire to expand his fund of knowledge, we can assume that he took side-trips while in Switzerland to visit landscapes, botanical gardens, and renew acquaintances with old friends as well as to meet new ones.

This was the last time Jacob was to visit Europe, and the last time he saw his mother who was then seventy-two years old. Mrs. Weidenmann was a strong, healthy woman. She would live another twenty-one years, out-living her son by six months.

By November 1871, Weidenmann was back in Hartford to face an unexpected string of bad luck. He naively hoped to resume his position of superintendent of both the City Park and Cedar Hill Cemetery, but much to his surprise, neither position was open to him.

On November 4, 1871, Weidenmann wrote about his plight to his friend and colleague Frederick Law Olmsted. Through their collaboration on the landscape for the Retreat in Hartford, a professional friendship had emerged between them. In his letter Weidenmann said:

> I am presently no where engaged. The members of the Board of Park Commissioners are with one exception, elected while I was in Europe and it seems that I have to ask for reinstatement as Superintendent. On Cedar Hill Cemetery I am needed very much, but also have trouble with Mr. Jacobs [Ward B. Jacobs], ticket agent, who is secretary and who had the whole management of C.H. Cemetery during my stay, he does not like my coming back and treated me very ungentlemanlike.

Obviously, Weidenmann was devastated. He had spent most of his savings on his sojourn in Switzerland, and was trying to reestablish himself to earn a living to support his family of five. He was hurt by the lack of gratitude shown by these two Boards after he had worked against difficult financial and political odds to see the City Park completed, and had succeeded in just five years to plan and execute the installation of the large ornamental foreground at Cedar Hill, as well as to construct the long entrance drive, and lay out several of the burial sections beyond.

No one is certain of the reasons these Boards so soundly rejected him. Some speculate that they did not like that he had taken such a long leave. Others suppose that the Boards did not approve his having developed a private practice that might distract him from his work for them, though there is no evidence that it did. Some believe that Weidenmann had grown impatient with these Board members who, because they controlled the purse strings, felt they knew more about landscape architecture than he did, all of which led to tensions between them prior to his leave. We do not know the real cause.

No doubt Weidenmann had a few private commissions to see him through, but the times were difficult. The country was getting back on course after the Civil War, but inflation was rampant and politics were corrupt. There was reckless speculation in the stock market especially relating to railroads, and there was over expansion in almost every field of endeavor, all which led to the Great Panic of 1873. There was high unemployment and businesses were failing at the rate of over 6,000 per year.

More bad luck came Weidenmann's way in 1874, when foreclosure proceedings were instigated against him by the Hartford County Superior Court, and "he was cheated out of a house ...on Capitol Avenue," according to his daughter, Marguerite. He had previously been taken to the Court of Common Pleas by James G. Wells, a crockery manufacturer and real estate developer, who sought to attach Weidenmann's property for the sum of four hundred dollars. Weidenmann was required by the Court to pay this sum, but he obviously did not, hence, the foreclosure.

This was the last straw in Weidenmann's unwelcome return to Hartford. He began making plans to move his family to New York, where he had commenced his career as a landscape architect almost twenty years earlier.

In the interim between his return from Switzerland and his move to New York, Frederick Law Olmsted came to the rescue. He obviously had great respect for Weidenmann as expressed in a letter to another colleague, George E. Waring, Jr., the civil engineer who had collaborated on the Retreat and other projects. He wrote: "I think well of Weidenmann and work with him better than with other landscape architects."

Weidenmann was then invited to go to New York to assist Olmsted and Vaux on the development of Prospect Park in Brooklyn, which Weidenmann did for a brief period, apparently leaving his family behind in Hartford.

Olmsted also offered him the task of implementing the general plan for the estate of Cyrus Field, the merchant capitalist and promoter of the trans-Atlantic cable. Field's primary residence was in Gramercy Park in the City, but it was for the estate that Field was developing in Irvington-on-Hudson, New York, that Weidenmann completed the plans.

Another commission that Weidenmann executed for Olmsted and Vaux was for the grounds surrounding Sanford Oscar Greenleaf's new house in Springfield, Massachusetts. Jacob had completed his projects for Olmsted in New York, and he was back in Hartford now, so the Greenleaf project was convenient being that Springfield was a short distance away by train. He was instructed to present Mr. Greenleaf with a copy of the general plan for the site and explain it to him, which he did in May of 1872. He reported back to Olmsted that Greenleaf liked the plan, but wanted to relocate a section of the drive in order to save a recently planted elm tree. As a result of visiting the site, Weidenmann made other suggestions to Olmsted and Vaux, such as widening the driveway so that the butcher and grocer could pass by a carriage parked by the front entrance, and correcting other issues relating to the walk, curbing, and drainage near the front entrance of the residence. After the resolution of these points, he would draw a planting plan for the project.

Mr. Greenleaf and his wife, Mary O. Hitchcock Greenleaf, implemented these plans on Sumner Street in Springfield. He was a paper manufacturer and held the position of treasurer of the Holyoke Paper Company. Unfortunately, this property has been demolished.

Despite the unsettled decade of the seventies, and the Panic of 1873, Olmsted and Vaux had a relatively steady flow of work. In addition to some private commissions, there was Central Park, a project fraught with political issues as well as problems with uncooperative personnel. There was also tension between Frederick Law Olmsted and Calvert Vaux. Although they had collaborated for many years, there was always the underlying feeling, on the part of Vaux, that Olmsted was receiving all of the credit for these works even though Olmsted tried his best to set the record straight. This issue and probably some others brought them to dissolving their partnership "for reasons of mutual convenience" on October 18, 1872.

Weidenmann continued executing special projects for Olmsted after the dissolution. He worked on the re-landscaping of "Boscobel," in Montrose, New York. The mansion was built in 1804 by States

Morris Dyckman, a descendent of one of the founding families of New Amsterdam. By 1873, the owner was W. B. Ogden, who desiring to revise the sixty-five year old landscape, contacted Olmsted, who then turned the project over to Weidenmann. Completed planting plans were delivered on March 28, 1873.

While "Boscobel" stands today as a unique example of its neo-classical style, it is located fifteen miles north of its original site. To save it from destruction, it was moved to Garrison, New York, in 1957, and in the process any vestiges of the original landscape were lost.

Another significant project that Olmsted assigned to Weidenmann was the Elmira School grounds in Elmira, New York. With some of these projects, such as the Greenleaf site mentioned earlier, Olmsted worked out the general plan with the client. In the case of Elmira, it was Weidenmann's duty to do the preliminary studies, the general plan, drainage plan, planting plan, and other details, six sheets of drawings in all. Favorable reactions came at each step of planning from Mr. G. M. Diven, a practicing attorney who served on the School's building committee. In one letter he asked what Weidenmann would think of a ". . . sort of Porter's Lodge at the remote corner of the grounds for a Janitor's residence." We have no record of Weidenmann's response.

A Formal Alliance

By 1874 Olmsted and Weidenmann were collaborating on enough projects that it became necessary for Weidenmann to move permanently to New York City and for the two of them to agree upon a working arrangement. Weidenmann established his office at the same 110 Broadway address as Olmsted's. By 1875 his entire family was settled in the City at 207 East 57th Street. After several years, they would move north to 114 East 103rd Street.

On May 19, 1874, Olmsted sent a letter to Weidenmann that consisted of two major "propositions" based on previous discussions they had about this proposed alliance. Weidenmann was to sign the agreement if he approved of its final form. It read:

> Proposition 1st: That when I [Olmsted] have a commission in which I need your aid in the general design as in the preparation of drawings of a plan [,] you shall bear all office expenses. Your traveling expenses, if any occur, shall be returned to you, and you shall be entitled to one-half the

compensation I receive for the plan. The plan in this case to bear your name under mine as associated in the design. Proposition 2nd: That when I wish to make use of your office organization and conveniences for the fair copy and elaboration of a plan[,]the general design of which I have prepared[,] or for any office work not covered by the 1st proposition, you shall cause an exact account to be kept of the cost of the same in salaries or wages of your assistants employed upon it and all direct outlays on account of it and render the same to me and shall be entitled to payment of the same together with an addition, for the payment of your general expenses and your personal superintendence, of not less than 25% nor more than 50% on the amount of such salaries or wages and expenses; the percentage varying according to the difficulty of the work and the degree of personal attention to it required by you. The result of such work to be mine as if done solely in my private office, you acting not as an associate designer but as my adjutant.

Olmsted presented an example of how a bill should be made out, and then he continued:

My object in the proposed arrangement with you being to have the advantage of an office staff always ready without the trouble and expense of maintaining it solely for my private business. I propose also that if you accept these propositions you shall likewise agree that the arrangement shall not terminate except after four months notice.
Signed: Yours truly, Fred.Law Olmsted.

Weidenmann took his time in responding, probably because he was away working on one of their mutual projects. When he did respond on June 1, 1874, his message was brief:

In answer to your proposition…I hereby approve and accept your schedule for a mutual business operation with the exception that the commission in your second proposition shall be not less than 25%, nor more than 100% on the actual expenses for material and time of myself and assistants.
Signed: Yours truly, J. Weidenmann.

Even before Olmsted formally sent his propositions to Weidenmann, probably after their preliminary discussion, Olmsted prepared a notice to be sent out and posted:

Mr. Olmsted's personal service is often asked with reference to the improvement of private grounds at times when his duties on public works compel him to decline proposed engagements for the purpose. Under these circumstances, Mr. Weidenmann, at the request of the applicants, sometimes acts in consultation with him and [provides] whatever is required under advice and review. The result in these cases having been particularly satisfactory to all concerned an alliance has been made by which the joint services in like manner of Mr. Olmsted and Mr. Weidenmann can at all times be commanded for any business of their common profession. May 14, 1874.

Both gentlemen took particular care not to use the word partnership for their new working arrangement. A partnership would imply that they shared equally in all aspects of operation: expenses, profits, liabilities, and all business related to the operation of their firm. Their written alliance was more limited in scope. It simply meant that Weidenmann would be available to assist Olmsted when needed, and spelled out how he would be compensated.

During the years following this agreement, Olmsted's commissions greatly increased. In many cases, though the initial contact with the client may have been made by him, he would often turn the whole project over to Weidenmann without commencing work on any of the plans, or even visiting the site in question. The alliance between these two landscape architects progressed smoothly, and it continued for the next nineteen years, until Weidenmann's death in 1893. However, after Olmsted moved his office to Brookline, Massachusetts in 1883 (to be nearer his extensive work in the Boston area), and after his son John joined the firm in 1884, there was less work for Weidenmann. By this time, however, Weidenmann's own private practice had grown.

The Charles A. Dana Villa Park
Oyster Bay, Long Island, New York

As early as 1873, Charles Anderson Dana (1819–1897) had asked Olmsted to visit and evaluate a tract of land he hoped to purchase in order to build "a number of villa sites, or sort of park," a residential subdivision in today's parlance. Olmsted turned the project over to Weidenmann who immediately drew a plan showing the lot arrangement as well as the road and drainage system. The project was on Dosoris Island, on the north shore of Long Island, in the town of Oyster Bay.

Dana planned to develop the tract to turn a profit, but he also wanted to reserve one of the best sites to build a villa for himself. He had spent an active and varied life, starting out as one of the early inhabitants of George Ripley's failed Utopian experiment at Brook Farm, in West Roxbury, Massachusetts. He later became managing editor of the *New York Tribune*, where he was its abolitionist voice and where he clashed with Horace Greeley. Eventually, he would become editor and part-owner of the *New York Sun* but not before serving first as Lincoln's "eyes" at the front during the Civil War, and later as Assistant Secretary of War under Secretary Edwin Stanton. He also edited the *New American Encyclopedia*, as well as the *American Encyclopedia*, and he wrote several books as well. This heavy work schedule prompted him to want a place where he might escape to create attractive grounds and collect "a remarkable variety of foreign [exotic] trees, shrubs, and flowers." In fact, he considered himself enough of a horticulturist to write "Conifers and Their Culture" for the 4 April 1888 issue of *Garden and Forest*.

Dana was a man who did not mince words or thoughts, probably a result of his years of writing and editing. Even though Olmsted had turned the project over to Weidenmann, Dana wrote to Olmsted about the plans saying that he thought the road plan "appears superfluous," but that in general the plan was satisfactory. He then went on to ask when Wisedell would have the plans for his house ready, "that being the pivot of the whole thing." Thomas Wisedell was a young English architect who collaborated with Calvert Vaux on the design of some of the buildings in Prospect Park, Brooklyn, and other projects.

The project eventually came to a conclusion, and though the Villa Park as originally laid out no longer remains, some of the villas are extant.

Masquetux, The Estate of Henry B. Hyde
Bay Shore, Long Island, New York

Across the spine of Long Island, on its South Shore, overlooking Great South Bay, Olmsted was invited to draw plans for a large estate for Henry B. Hyde (1834–1899), who founded the Equitable Life Assurance Society in New York City at the very young age of twenty-five. The year was 1874, and Olmsted immediately turned the project over to Weidenmann who conceived the design and executed the working plans for the transformation of over one hundred acres into a private residential estate. Despite his constant complaints about costs, Hyde apparently was pleased with the results.

The generally rectangular and gently undulating site included a vale containing a wetland in the center. Weidenmann created one large and four small free-form lakes here and these became a focal point on the estate, second only to the large and expansive stick-style mansion, designed by Calvert Vaux. Vaux and Olmsted, still friends, continued to collaborate on certain projects with Vaux executing the building plans.

The property was divided in the manner of the times, with the house set well back from the main road on flat land having the best prospect, with a pleasing lawn and pleasure ground surrounding it. Supportive farm buildings, an orchard, and vegetable gardens were in the rear of the property. An extensive road and path system connected these parts of the landscape physically, while strong lines-of-vista connected them visually where desired.

The road and path system required much planning to address both plan layout and drainage considerations. On the western side of the estate the main drive led directly to the mansion, curving slightly in order to make the vista to the mansion unfold with the visitor's progression. This drive, relatively short, split into an oval-shaped turn-around in front of the main entrance of the mansion, to surround a large lawn panel in the center. The drive then continued, in a gentle curve, to the rear of the property in order to serve the barns and gardens.

On the east side of the estate, a second drive, this one more winding, crossed a bridge at the lake and offered numerous vistas across open lawns, and up the wooded vale to the north. Branching off this drive, two secondary drives led through the grounds to the north, and encircled the lakes and the dale, and off these drives extended a sinuous system of footpaths. This entire southeast section of the estate was a virtual park, with a combination of woods and open fields, while the eastern part consisted of lawns and pleasure grounds near the house.

The lawns surrounding the mansion were extensive. The smaller one was within the circular drive mentioned above, but then there was a large, heart-shaped lawn defined by the drive and paths on the south side of the mansion that afforded magnificent views of the lake, or of the mansion from the lake road, depending on one's vantage point. On the east side of the house was a circular lawn, half of which was flat for playing croquet, but the portion that sloped towards the dale was planted with a grove of trees.

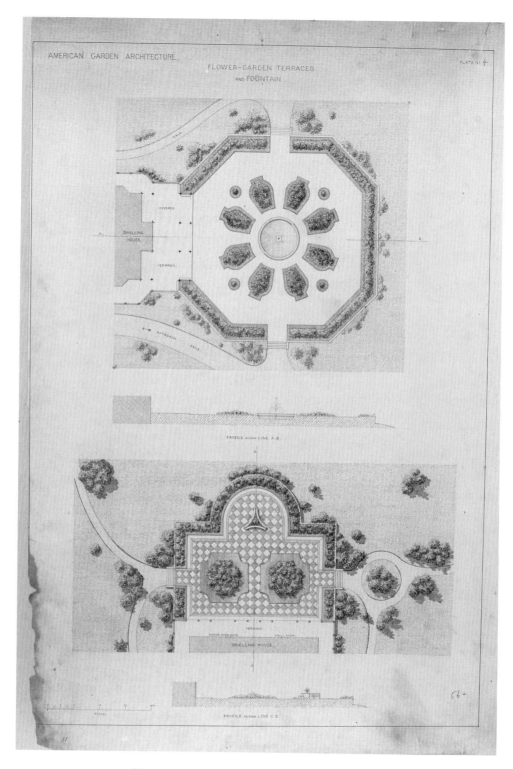

Plans for two garden terraces. Top, "Masquetux";
bottom, Charles Dana residence. From *American Garden Architecture.*

The landscape plan for "Masquetux," drawn by Jacob Weidenmann.
From Edouard Andre's *Parcs et Jardins* (1879).

To the rear of the mansion, the road and a gravel walk defined a half-circle lawn, leading through gardens at intervals along the way. This space was enclosed by shrub plantings in order to provide seasonal beauty, but also to create an intimate ornamental garden space. A pavilion with appended pergolas framed the north side of this garden.

Across the rear of the estate two barns stood, one on each side of the property, with a large vegetable garden between them laid out in a highly symmetrical pattern in contrast to the natural style of the ornamental landscape. An octagonal poultry house formed the centerpiece of this complex. A large orchard of between fifty and sixty trees made the transition from the farm complex to the park, and it also served as a screening buffer.

The entire estate was planted with hundreds of trees and shrubs, all carefully placed to enclose and define the various spaces, and to create the wooded park within the dale. Trees were also carefully placed to frame and emphasize vistas from one part of the estate to another.

The landscaping of "Masquetux" continued for several years. Mr. Hyde was a reasonable but demanding client, and though Weidenmann was in charge of the planning, Hyde often contacted Olmsted for approval and with questions about billing. We know that the plans for "Masquetux" were completed by 1876 because that year Weidenmann exhibited them in a competitive exhibit at the Centennial Exhibition in Philadelphia. The award judges presented him with a "Medal and Diploma for the Best System and Most Instructive Plans and Specifications for Practically Improving and Embellishing Grounds, Survey, Drainage, Planting, and general Map for Improving 'Masquetux' on Long Island, Unanimously Awarded to J. Weidenmann, Landscape Architect."

By studying the plan for "Masquetux," it is easy to see why the judges awarded Weidenmann the winning "Medal and Diploma." The sinuosity of his drive and walk system, which evolved from the natural contours of the land, the water features provided by nature, and the intervening spaces produced by the design of that system, all combined to create a beautifully organic plan, based entirely upon the dictates of nature, while still meeting the clients multi-faceted demands for the site. Designing with nature is the basis of the landscape architecture profession today, and a concept that all professionals in the field attempt to follow.

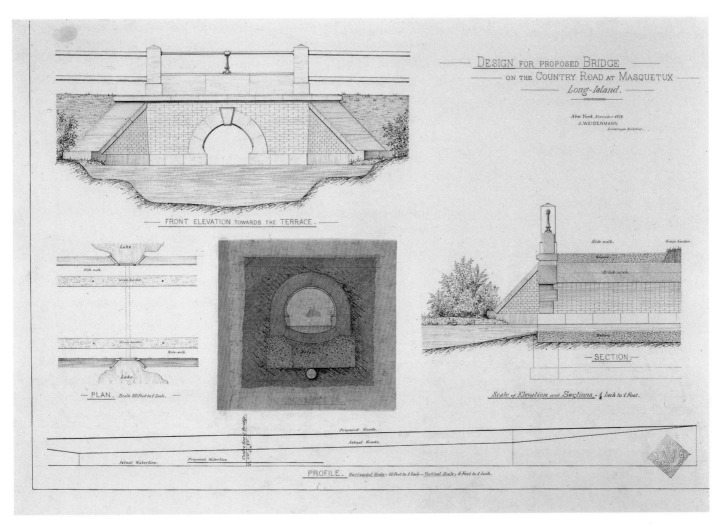

DESIGN FOR PROPOSED BRIDGE
ON THE COUNTRY ROAD AT MASQUETUX
Long-Island.

New-York, November 1874.
J. WEIDENMANN
Landscape Architect.

— FRONT ELEVATION TOWARDS THE TERRACE. —

— PLAN. Scale 20 Feet to 1 Inch. —

— SECTION —

Scale of Elevation and Sections. ¼ Inch to 1 Foot.

PROFILE. Horizontal Scale = 10 Feet to 1 Inch — Vertical Scale = 5 Feet to 1 Inch.

Plan for the stone bridge for the county road, "Masquetux",
designed by Weidenmann. From *American Garden Architecture*.

Weidenmann also received another honor for his work at "Masquetux." In 1879, when the landscape was virtually completed, a book was published in France that featured this project as an excellent example of the picturesque style in America. The book was written by Edouard Andre' and was entitled *L'Art des Jardins, Traite' General de la Composition des PARCS ET JARDIN*. Several pages are devoted to Weidenmann's plan with examples of his enhancement of views, and the arrangement of trees and shrubs to achieve particular effects, as well as many other details. Olmsted was an acquaintance of Andre', and they visited while Olmsted was in Paris. They talked about American examples to include in the book, and corresponded later, and this example was certainly suggested.

Most of the Masquetux mansion still stands, though greatly altered, and it is now the Southward Ho Country Club. What remains of the ninety acre estate has been transformed into an 18 hole, par 71, golf course.

Four Government Buildings
United States Capitol, Washington, D.C.

Frederick Law Olmsted began working on landscape plans for the United States capitol grounds in the spring of 1874, and the project continued for the rest of the decade and into the next. It was a large and involved project, covering about fifty acres surrounding the Capitol, and for this reason he relied on Weidenmann's assistance in executing the plans at the start. At this time, Olmsted's work was expanding, so having a reliable associate such as Weidenmann was a great help. Unlike some former projects, Olmsted kept the lead on this one, using Weidenmann as his trusted "adjutant."

The first phase of this work was the East Front for which Weidenmann drew the general plan based on concepts and rough sketches they had made. After this plan was agreed upon, Olmsted asked him to provide a watercolor rendering of it for presentation purposes, an art in which Weidenmann excelled. After the acceptance of the general plan by the Senate Committee on Public Grounds, headed by Senator Justin Morrill of Vermont, Weidenmann set to work drawing the grading and drainage plan for the site in collaboration with the team's civil engineers. He then worked closely with Olmsted in solving the severe drainage problems, brought about by the compaction of the heavy clay soil during construction of the Capitol building. This involved deep plowing and the incorporation of quantities of organic matter to make the soil friable and suitable for lawn, tree, and shrub planting.

The "Masquetux" poultry house and aviary, designed by Jacob Weidenmann.
From *American Garden Architecture*.

Work on the East Front landscape commenced in the spring of 1874, and by late autumn of that year, the ground was ready for final treatment. The East Front landscape, as well as the rest of the Capitol Grounds, has been transformed many times in the one-hundred-thirty years since this original plan, and as this is being written, Olmsted's East Front landscape is threatened again with the construction of a visitor center and security devices.

United States Quartermaster Depot, Jeffersonville, Indiana.

Quartermaster General Montgomery C. Meigs designed the United States Quartermaster's Depot, across the Ohio River from Louisville, Kentucky, and its construction was completed in early 1874. It was a large project, covering four city blocks with the buildings around the outside of the complex forming a large open space in the center. The buildings were well designed, constructed of brick, and one architectural historian labeled the 2.7 million cubic foot structure as "functional architecture of the highest quality."

In the spring of 1874, Olmsted was contacted by Meigs to draw a plan for landscaping the courtyard, pointing out that although shrub plantings were desired, lines of vision to every door within the complex had to be clear for the guard on duty.

Olmsted turned this project over to Weidenmann. A plan entitled: "Planting Map for the Cortile [Courtyard]" was completed in April of 1874. At the cortile's center he designed a large rosette parterre consisting of eight compartments heavily planted with low-growing shrubs. Each compartment was separated from the next by a sidewalk, and these walks continued to the outer perimeter of the cortile. Very little planting is shown for the perimeter presumably to keep lines-of-sight open as requested.

Weidenmann executed this project quickly after making a site visit at its inception. On May 20, 1874, General Meigs wrote to Olmsted indicating his pleasure with "the admirable design with drawings," but because of the closing of the fiscal year, he could not send payment until the new fiscal year started in July. Plans for this project remain on file at the National Archives and Records Administration, in Washington, D. C.

Another government project initiated in 1875 was the re-landscaping of the Schuylkill Arsenal, built in 1800. Over the years, the Arsenal was expanded, and the grounds were in need of reorganization. Olmsted assigned Weidenmann to this project, though there were many other experts involved including civil engineers and surveyors.

Olmsted asked Weidenmann to do preliminary studies for the site, work with the surveyor, Mr. William Davies, and civil engineer, George Radford, on drainage issues, to develop a contract and cost estimate to present to Mr. Stewart VanVliet, Assistant Quartermaster General, and then to develop the plans for executing the work. The detailed planning was initiated by Olmsted and Weidenmann on July 26, 1875. Total costs for the proposed work were estimated at fifteen thousand dollars (about $222,000 today).

In the subsequent months, Weidenmann completed preliminary studies, and from these the general plan for improvement was drawn. Upon approval of this plan, he worked with Radford to complete extensive grading and drainage plans. Plans and specifications were also drawn for the entrance gateway lodge, gates, and additions and improvements to the officers' quarters, and the final planting plan. The streetcar tracks were relocated as part of this project, running from Gray's Ferry Road to Warehouse Number 3, and because this was a revision of the original plan, it caused some problems relating to the original cost estimate which included neither moving the track nor the bluestone edging that was to define the area. After considerable correspondence, this issue was finally resolved.

This large project required many visits to the site by Weidenmann, not only to gather data for drawing the plans, but also to work with the surveyor in staking out the plans on the ground once they were drawn. The project was completed in 1876. At this writing, the building still exists, though transformed, and the 1874 landscape is no longer evident.

Hot Springs Reservation, Arkansas

Jacob Weidenmann's business announcement of the early 1880s lists in fine print his most recent completed works. Among them is the Hot Springs Reservation, with the date 1878. This was a significant year for the Reservation because the United States Government was deciding what it would retain of this vast holding, and what it would sell off. Though the Government had owned the site since 1832, they were just beginning to take active interest in its administration.

Between 1877 and 1878, Frederick A. Clark was the chief engineer for the site, and during this period he wrote several letters to the Olmsted firm in New York. At one point, Mr. Clark made a trip to New York to talk about the Hot Springs site. Apparently, Frederick Law Olmsted turned the project over to Weidenmann, but there is no record of what he did there. He may have advised on the subdivision of the land, but it is most likely that he drew plans for the "government free bathhouses" and their siting, since these were built at this time.

Today, nothing remains at Hot Springs that dates from this 1878 period. Massive changes that transformed all earlier work were made by the Olmsted firm in 1892, but Weidenmann was not involved with this phase of work.

Congress Park
Saratoga Springs, New York

Saratoga Springs was named for the several springs around which the town was founded. As early as 1810, Dr. John Clarke boarded a ten-foot square area around one of them, and then erected an awning over the boardwalk so that people coming to drink the waters would be shielded from the sun or rain. By 1835, an elaborate Doric temple had been constructed over the spring. At about this same time, "swamp walks" were built in the wet land surrounding the springs, the beginnings of a small park for visitors. Between 1812 and 1826 there was a bottling plant situated near the springs so that the healthful water could be sold to the public not taking the waters at the source.

The springs were a great attraction not only to residents of Saratoga Springs, but also to visitors who came on vacation during the summer months, staying at local boarding houses and hotels.

In 1875, Frederick Law Olmsted was asked by the Trustees of the Congress and Empire Spring Company to produce a plan to enlarge the small park that would utilize the entire thirty-four acres that had been acquired over the years. The site was difficult because of the wet, swampy land surrounding the springs and an incline towards rugged ground that drained into these wetlands. Olmsted agreed to take on the project, and he immediately turned the site planning over to Weidenmann.

The Central Fountain, Congress Park, soon after completion, Saratoga Springs, New York.

Weidenmann, well trained in engineering as well as design, was challenged. He first drew a general plan, and then a grading plan on which he showed the creation of three ponds, with a system of sinuous walks weaving between them and interconnecting the various spaces in the park. A deer park was also included. Planting plans provided for specimen trees throughout the park, with masses of shrubs sited to surround spaces within the park and to frame vistas. The perimeter of the park was heavily planted with groves of trees buffering the park from the city.

At the edge of the lower and largest lake, Weidenmann designed and sited an elegant music pavilion where concerts could be given on Sunday afternoons, or even at other special times. The stand was octagonal with an intricate mosaic tile floor. Delicate cast iron columns supported the elegant roof, oriental in design. From the ceiling was suspended an elaborate chandelier especially designed to conform to the fine tracery of the cast iron brackets supporting the roof. On each column were candelabras, probably gas-lighted, so that evening concerts could be held in summer. During the first year, Hall's Boston Band held forth, and in subsequent years, Downing's New York Band, and Brown's Brigade Band of Boston performed.

As landscape work in the Park was nearing completion, new work commenced on an arcade just within the main Park entrance. Calvert Vaux and his partner Frederick C. Withers were asked to design a large structure to cover and connect Congress and Columbia Springs. Their plan showed an enclosed pavilion over each of the springs, and these were connected with long arcades, with trellises at intervals, for which Weidenmann specified Woodbines *(Parthenocissus quinquefolia)*, an American native. Within the arcades were a café and vending stands.

Completed plans were presented to the trustees of the Park on July 12, 1875, after which Weidenmann worked very closely with Mr. Dawson, the local surveyor-engineer, who laid out the drainage work. In June of 1876, the *Daily Saratogian* reported:

> The 'welcome' and the cheer are never doubtful. Congress Park has undergone a transformation, which will make the eyes of the old visitors stick out with wonder and satisfaction. It will be a little world in itself, and be regarded as one of *the* features of Saratoga this centennial year. Indeed the entire place has been putting on its 'best bib and tucker' on account of our one Hundredth birthday . . . We are ready to show the world what a real enterprising nation can do in the way of mineral springs accommodations for 'man and beast' in the short space of one hundred years.

·PUBLIC PARK·

View of Congress Park. The Olmsted-Weidenmann designed portion
is on the right; Calvert Vaux's pavilion in the right foreground.

MUSIC PAVILION.

ELEVATION.

PLAN.

Jacob Weidenmann's design for the Music Pavilion
built at Congress Park. From *American Garden Architecture*.

Today, 130 years after this newspaper account, Congress Park is preserved and enjoyed by Saratoga Springs' residents and tourists. The music pavilion and the arcades are gone, but most of the other landscape features remain.

Cornell University
Ithaca, New York

In the spring of 1874, Andrew Dickson White, first president of Cornell University, asked Jacob Weidenmann to do a plan for the campus including the new Sage College that was nearing completion. Weidenmann was not the first to be asked to make a master plan for this nine-year-old University. Five other planners had been asked before him, including Frederick Law Olmsted, and White had rejected all of their plans.

Obviously, President White had strong ideas for what he wanted on the new campus. In his autobiography, he mentioned coming across a book, while a freshman in college, in which he read about Oxford and Cambridge and their King's, Merton, Magdalen, and other colleges, all laid out in quadrangles. He wrote that later in life, "in the midst of all other occupations I was constantly rearing these structures on that queenly site above the finest of the New York lakes, and dreaming of a university worthy of the commonwealth and the nation. This dream became a sort of obsession..." An obsession it was, and because of it, he rejected any plan that would not conform to his firm ideas.

Weidenmann went to Ithaca on May 3, 1874, to analyze the site and make notes for future planning. President White told him where he wanted the roads laid out, where he should put the botanical garden, and how they wanted the farm complex designed. Of utmost importance was an immediate plan for the grounds around the new Sage College, donated by Henry W. Sage, which was nearing completion as the first college for women students within a university anywhere in the United States. White wanted this portion of the plans immediately so that the College could be landscaped by commencement.

After two days of making site studies at Cornell, Weidenmann went back to his office in New York to work on the plan. It wasn't long before White wrote to him asking why he had not received the plan for Sage College. Weidenmann responded that he would not do the plan for the College as a separate piece, and that he had to sketch out the entire campus plan first before developing the details for the

The Albert Thorvaldsen cast iron urns of the early 1800s,
entitled "Day and Night," Congress Park.

Sage College. "No man of sense would do it" he wrote back to White. He explained that he was "trying to submit . . . a plan of practical suggestions bringing in harmony all the different features of the ground and particularly bear in mind the future extent and demand of the Institution, as I believe that satisfactory results can only be obtained by correct principals and sound reasons." Weidenmann then agreed to finish the plans in four days, and ship them on the 8th of June.

Knowing that President White would be unhappy that the Sage College plans had not been sent ahead, Weidenmann wrote in his June 8 letter that doing the master plan first, and then detailing the Sage College grounds, would save the University thousands of dollars in the long run, and "give satisfaction and credit to the managers" because they would not have to redo their work in the future.

Weidenmann's master plan suggested a new entrance to the campus, with a bridge over Cascadilla Gorge, and the main road then curving to the front of Sage College and approaching what was to become the major campus quadrangle in the center of its southern border. (Buildings were already built on only the west and north sides.) Then the road was to continue in a circular loop inside the quadrangle, allowing plenty of room between it and the buildings for an expanse of lawn and trees. On the west side of the few buildings that had been built, Weidenmann suggested a series of long terraces, obviously so that users could enjoy the spectacular views of Lake Cayuga from them, one of the finest views on any university campus. In effect, Weidenmann was turning inside out President White's quadrangle, which would have turned its back on the Lake.

His plan was soundly rejected in a scathing letter written by White on September 9, 1874, two months after it had been received. First of all, he scolded Weidenmann for getting the plans for Sage College there so late that they could not get the grounds landscaped before commencement. Then he told him that the entire plan was "impracticable," that the agriculture faculty did not like the farm layout, and that the botanical garden had not been sited where they wanted it. Furthermore, Weidenmann had not listened to them with regard to the roads, he wrote, and the plan "violated conditions which I had laid down."

After six pages of admonishments, White concluded by saying that he did not attribute the inadequacy of the plan to Weidenmann's lack of skill, and he would pay for all of the expenses incurred, but he was not "aware of any rule in law, morals, or honor which require more than this." He signed off by saying that he desired to remain "on friendly footing with you."

Weidenmann worked together with Olmsted on several projects by conducting site studies, developing plans, and assisting in any way necessary to expedite the work. He helped in drafting the initial plan for Mount Royal Park in Montreal, as well as drawing the general plan for Niagara Square in Buffalo, New York, and the extensive park system there. Another project on which he assisted was to design the grounds of Buffalo's New York Asylum for the Insane. Further south, in Baltimore, he worked on the general plan for Johns Hopkins University. These projects all occurred between 1876 and 1879.

During the 1870s he also drew plans for several private estates, at least two of them referred to him by Olmsted. They were the grounds for Mrs. James Cooper Lord's estate, in Morristown, New Jersey, where he developed a complete set of plans. Mrs. Lord found the plans "entirely satisfactory," except that Weidenmann misunderstood and drew plans for a stable and gardener's cottage as well, plans that Mrs. Lord already had had drawn by someone else, not knowing Weidenmann's proficiency in architecture.

Another Olmsted reference was for the Mathews mansion in Norwalk, Connecticut, today called the Lockwood-Mathews Mansion. It was built by LeGrand Lockwood in 1865, a grand stone villa complete with an attached conservatory in the style of the day.

Lockwood died just seven years afterwards, and in 1876, his widow sold the villa to Charles D. Mathews, a New York importer, whose family retained the estate until 1938. Mathews wished to complete the landscape and also to revise some of Lockwood's schemes for the site, which prompted his contacting Olmsted who apparently turned the project over to Weidenmann. The site was extensive, about thirty acres, complete with a large park and meadowland, stables, and gardens. Today the extensive grounds are greatly reduced and none of the details remain.

Weidenmann, on his own, had received commissions from several other New York businessmen, professionals, and politicians. He planned the estate of William Davis Shipman, in Astoria, New York. Shipman was a descendent of an old Connecticut family, and former United States District Judge for the district of Connecticut. After moving to New York, he became a partner in the law firm of Barlow, Larocque, and McFarland, in the city.

Lockwood-Mathews Mansion, Norwalk, Connecticut.

Study for a Watertower

Jacob Weidenmann

One concept designed and painted by Jacob Weidenmann, possibly for the belvedere at "Owl's Head."

There were also several estates along the Hudson River, as far north as Dobbs Ferry, for which Weidenmann laid out the grounds and drew planting plans. In Brooklyn, on Bay Ridge, along the present Shore Road, he planned the twenty-seven acre estate of Eliphalet Williams Bliss, a manufacturer. The place was called "Owl's Head Park," and it was indeed a park lavishly planted with trees and picturesque masses of shrubs, with a lawn that sloped to the Bay. The house was set on top of the ridge on a flat area. South of the mansion was a large observatory, or belvedere, designed by Weidenmann especially for the site. The views across The Narrows to Staten Island and the wooded shores of New Jersey were spectacular. Today the place is a public park, Bliss Park, and visitors may see the rise in the ground and the flat lawn where the belvedere and mansion once stood.

Up the River in Yonkers, Weidenmann laid out the grounds for Samuel Jones Tilden called "Greystone." A former governor of New York, and the democratic candidate for president of the United States in 1876 (who gained the popular vote, but lost by one electoral vote to Rutherford B. Hayes), Tilden had his main residence in Gramercy Park in the City, but he purchased "Greystone" in 1879, where he spent most of his retirement years. The mansion was built in 1864 by John T. Waring, a hat manufacturer. After purchasing it, Tilden altered the veranda and entrance portico, as well as the vast landscape surrounding the mansion that sloped to the shores of the Hudson River. The park surrounding the mansion followed Weidenmann's usual pattern of many trees and shrubs, and few flower gardens, strongly emphasizing natural views. "Greystone" is now a public park known as Greystone-Untermeyer Park, Untermeyer, a lawyer, having purchased the place in 1899.

According to his daughter, Marguerite Weidenmann, Jacob also drew complete landscape plans for three other clients in New Jersey. One was Stewart Hartshorn, inventor of the roller window shade, who developed a residential park called "Short Hills" in Millburn Township, New Jersey. Hartshorn had no patience for "chain store homes," or cookie-cutter plans for siting them. He wanted a residential park, featuring the natural landscape enhanced by additional plantings, with each house designed in a different style, mainly Stick-Style, Shingle-Style, Queen Anne, Colonial Revival, Craftsman, and English Tudor. Weidenmann advised on the planning of this development, but it is not known if his advice took the form of written reports, working plans, or just stand-up consultations.

Weidenmann had another New Jersey client, Colonel Sweeting L. Miles. He drew plans for Miles's estate, which was along the Palisades Boulevard, in Bergen County. The plans have not been found except for a gate design, which he specified should be built of Sassafras wood instead of Cedar because it "will give much more satisfaction as regards its appearance, after the wear and tear of a few years."

Another project was the Villard Houses (now incorporated into The New York Palace Hotel at 451–457 Madison Avenue, New York). As Joseph Wells, an architect employed by the well-known firm of McKim, Meade, and White, was drawing plans for the Villard Houses, Weidenmann was working on plans for the landscaping of their courtyard. Henry Villard, the railroad entrepreneur, had the houses designed in a U-shape, modeled after the Palazzo della Cancelleria in Rome. Today, neither the courtyard nor Weidenmann's plans remain.

Chapter Six

Midwest: Iowa and Chicago

Weidenmann had many commissions after he moved his office to New York City and became affiliated with Olmsted; however, he was concerned that they were plentiful only when the economy was strong, but scarce when it was weak. In other words, the jobs piled up when times were good, but when the economy fell, few were available. This is a condition that artists have confronted since the beginning of time. He wrote to his friend Olmsted in May 1876 that he was concerned about always having to make a living "by our profession" continuously dependent upon the "fluctuations of the general business world."

He decided that he needed to expand the geographical range of his practice to cover a region beyond the New York City region. Perhaps he made this decision knowing that Olmsted was planning to move his office to Brookline, Massachusetts, as he did in 1883, in order to be closer to his ever-expanding Boston work. Weidenmann thought that being known in a wider sphere would be helpful when it inevitably came time to deal with the vicissitudes of the economy.

State Capitol Building
Des Moines, Iowa

Somehow Weidenmann heard about a competition for the design of the new Iowa State Capitol grounds in Des Moines and decided to apply. He became one of three being considered, and was finally selected as the landscape architect. The other applicants were a Mr. Carpenter, from Galesburg, Illinois, and Albert N. Prentiss, professor of botany at Cornell University, who had also drawn a plan for the campus there that was rejected by President Andrew Dickson White prior to Weidenmann's. The selection process commenced on September 6, 1884, the applicants' proposals were submitted by December 18, and Weidenmann signed a contract for the work on February 25, 1885.

He started the project immediately, creating a set of plans consisting of preliminary studies, a topographic plan, the general plan showing how the grounds surrounding the capitol would be developed, and drainage and grading plans. These plans were completed by July of 1885, and he then began immediately on detailed plans for the walks and drives, including their construction details, and also on the planting plans, all of which he presented on December 15. To these drawings, he added written reports concerning the drainage and planting schemes. At the request of the Grounds Committee of the

Iowa General Assembly, he also presented an estimate of construction costs for the project, which came to $130,786.11 (approximately $2,764,816.00 today). The development of these plans necessitated several trips back and forth to Des Moines from his office in New York.

The capitol building, begun in 1873 and completed in 1884, was sited on a high rise of ground at the east end of a four-acre tract. The central corridor of the building, and the majestic steps on both the east and west fronts, were on axis with Locust Street on the west and Capitol Avenue of the east. This square site was framed by Ninth, Eleventh, Sycamore, and Walnut Streets. The ground from the west steps of the Capitol sloped forty feet down to Ninth Street, and this change in elevation gave the building a commanding prospect. Weidenmann chose to emphasize this advantage in the development of his plans.

First, however, he addressed the matter of vehicular access. Primary curving drives led to the east and west fronts of the building, while secondary ones, narrower in width, curved around the building to the north and south doors. These drives were gently curving in order to blend well with the contours of the land and also to accommodate the awkward turning radii of horse-drawn carriages.

Pedestrian walks lead to the building from these drives, but the main pedestrian approach to the west front, or city side of the building, was a magnificent stair plaza ascending the forty-foot slope from Ninth Street to the Capitol's west front. Pedestrians arrived by streetcar, or on foot, and ascended the eighty steps to the building level. If the steps were a problem, they could go around to the east front or approach the west front from the circular driveway.

Weidenmann's design for the stair plaza is a splendid example of form and function working in concert. From Ninth Street, the forty foot wide staircase is broken with two major terraces, as well as two additional comfortable landings. The lower terrace is forty feet square, and the upper one is a rectangle of about thirty-five by eighty feet. The size of these terraces varies not only for interest, but also to fit the natural grade of the slope. The sides of the stair plaza are defined by a low, elegantly coped, granite wall.

This plaza, on axis with the Capitol's main corridor, and the highly symmetrical arrangement of driveways and walks, divided the lawn area into fifteen sections, which Weidenmann skillfully unified with his planting plan, repeating like masses in the various sections, and placing groves of trees to straddle some sections in a manner that would visually tie one section to the next.

Weidenmann had three objectives in executing his drainage plan: dealing with surface water, creating a system to carry it off, and laying agricultural tile below ground to drain certain areas. An extensive system of catch basins was designed for the surface water, and these were placed along walks and drives, on the terrace platforms, and at the edges of the lawn behind walls. These basins were connected to an underground system of vitrified pipes, which then flowed into the city sewer system. In his written comments accompanying his plans, Weidenmann points out most emphatically the importance of burying the lines safely below frost level. The drainage system also included underground pipes so that wet areas could be made suitable for the proper growth of lawns, shrubs, and trees.

Written comments accompanying his drainage and grading plans were extensive. He developed plans for the construction of catch basins, turf gutters, manholes, and inspection holes for the lines, along with comments which described the care to be taken when laying the gas lines to serve the candelabras (lamp posts), and the importance of not running these lines under planting beds or in other areas where they might be disturbed. All of these descriptions were written in Weidenmann's precise penmanship, and with great clarity. Here is an example:

> Gas pipes for the illumination of the approaches and walks should be laid in the lawn running parallel with the walk edging or curb and about 12 inches off from it enough to avoid the interfering with the silt basin. Leaky gas pipes destroy trees, shrubs, and grass for a distance of ten or more feet according to the character of the soil. For this reason the lines chosen for gas pipes should be of the shortest distance to the top of the Candelabrums at the same time avoiding to pass under trees and shrubs.

The Grounds Committee, anxious to improve the rough ground around the new Capitol, and smooth out the mounds of soil and ruts from construction, prepared to put the work out to bid. Meanwhile Weidenmann continued work on the planting plans. By September 1885, contractor Hugh King, along with his thirty-seven workmen and fifty horse teams, started executing the plans, working diligently throughout the autumn to complete the work before winter. They met their goal for the area immediately surrounding the Capitol Building by November 9. The stair plaza was not part of this contract.

Iowa State Capitol, Des Moines.

Weidenmann completed the planting plans shortly afterwards on December 15, 1885. They were extensive, comprising many sheets, organized so that each page showed one of the fifteen sections that fell between two walks, or between the walks and the structures, a natural way to divide the property for these purposes. He identified the plants by number, and the specifications for them appeared in a separate list of twenty-two pages, with an additional six pages of explanation. His presentation of the plans, plant specifications, and written descriptions are clear and concise, and could serve as a model to this day to students learning the profession.

The plant lists comprised 29 evergreens, 242 specimen shade trees, and 3,474 shrubs. These included popular plants that we now associate with the late 19th Century: white and Engelmann firs, Austrian pines, catalpas, maples, oaks, tulip trees, ash, lindens, magnolias, hawthorns, and Osage oranges. For the shrubs, there were various spiraeas, flowering quince, snowberries, weigelas, mock orange, deutzias, glossy sumac, fringe trees, hydrangeas, red-stemmed dogwoods, and Tartarian honeysuckle, to name but a few.

While many of these plants are the same as those recommended in his book, *Beautifying Country Homes*, for various other projects, certain plants, such as the Osage orange, were added to meet Iowa's hardiness requirements. In his written comments, Weidenmann was careful to point out that he had consulted with Messrs. C.L. Watrous of Des Moines, Mr. R. Douglas of Waukegan, Illinois, Mr. P.J. Peterson of Rosehill near Chicago, and Mr. M.R. Sloan of Grange, Illinois. Presumably, these men were either nurserymen, or experienced gardeners.

Weidenmann was explicit in stating his objectives for the planting plans:

> In preparing the planting Map my aim was chiefly directed to a composition which will help to increase the picturesque effect of the Capitol-building in time when the principal trees are more fully developed. However, I must say that it is extremely difficult to do full justice to every vista by mere studying of the Maps and sections without natural proportions of perspective and skyline before the composer, and that it would be desirable to verify the arrangements on the ground when the plantings have been staked out.

This is a statement that has been made many times over by landscape architects especially when they design projects from afar.

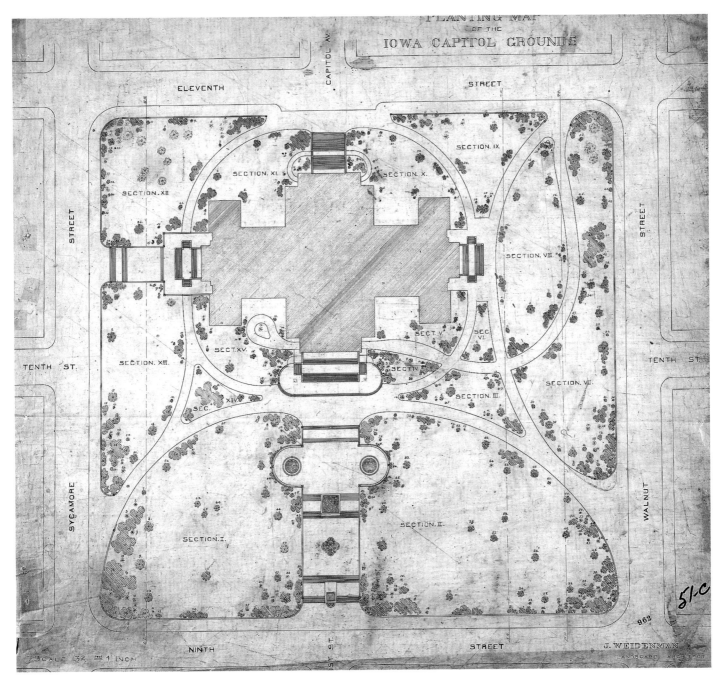

Jacob Weidenmann's planting plan for the Iowa State Capitol, Des Moines.

It is clear in studying his "arrangements" of plants that he was trying to achieve several major goals. As mentioned previously, he used groves of trees and masses of shrubs, repeated in the various sections, to unify the whole site, though he emphasizes the importance of "as much uninterrupted lawn surface as possible" as a unifying element. Shade trees were strategically placed to frame vistas, or as accents in the lawn. The evergreens created picturesque effects, along with contrasting shrub masses. Other shrub masses were also placed to define spaces within the landscape and also to buffer Capitol Square from the outside streets. Within the masses was an interplay of color, foliage texture, and plant form to create interest.

Concluding his twenty-eight page specifications and comments for the planting plan, Weidenmann seized the opportunity, as he often did, to sing the praises of landscape architecture as an art:

> In conclusion, I wish to say . . . that landscape gardening is an art having due place side by side with Poetry, Architecture, Music, Painting, and Sculpture for nearly two centuries our greatest and most popular teachers — as Sir Walter Scott for example — have given that rank, its influence upon the average populations is even stronger than Poetry, Music, and Painting on account of its realization in nature and for this reason the importance of introducing at the Capitol Grounds the choicest collection of ornamental trees and shrubs consistent with the climate and temperature can not be over estimated and I am in hope these limited grounds around the Capitol of Iowa to be the beginning of a school of art and culture in this direction.

It is not certain how much of the planting plan was implemented in 1886. Certainly the portions surrounding the stair plaza, sections I and II were not; the plaza was not completed until five years afterwards, and planting would not have been done until the plaza was completed so that the drainage and grading surrounding it could be installed.

Probably due to budget constraints, Weidenmann was asked to delay drawing detailed plans for the construction of the Grand Stair Plaza. It was not until August 25, 1890, that work began on this phase. On that date, the George Green and Company Quarry, in South Thomaston, Maine, was awarded the bid to provide 12,000 cubic feet of granite for the stairs. James B. Locke of Des Moines contracted to haul the granite from the train depot when it arrived, and make the footings and to start setting the first courses of the foundations.

Weidenmann's work for the State Capitol was well received, and as a result he was asked to advise on several other projects, one of them being the design of a residential park on forty-five acres "of a most unfavorable undulation of high priced land . . . ," though "overlooking as pretty scenery as can be found anywhere outside the grand scenery of mountainous country." The tract was high above the Raccoon River.

A mansion had already been built in the northeastern section of this land by Benjamin Franklin Allen, sixteen years before Weidenmann began work on this project in 1885. The place, called "Terrace Hill," was considered the "finest mansion west of the Mississippi." Shortly after it was built in 1869, Allen hired Job T. Elletson, an English landscape gardener from Rochester, New York, to plan a landscape of extensive gardens, a deer park, a pond, and a large conservatory. The mansion was set on a carpet of lawn amongst shade trees on the highest prospect looking south towards the river and north to Greenwood Avenue.

Benjamin Franklin Allen was considered the richest man in Des Moines, and in 1874 he purchased the Cook County National Bank in Chicago. Unfortunately, twelve months later, he went bankrupt, and eventually "Terrace Hill" had to be sold. A successful Des Moines real estate broker, Frederick Marion Hubbell, purchased "Terrace Hill" and the seven acres surrounding it for $60,000.00 in May of 1884 (over one million dollars today). He and his wife, Frances Cooper Hubbell, grandniece of the novelist James Fenimore Cooper, immediately moved into the mansion, and it was held by his descendents until 1971, when it then became the Iowa Governor's mansion, with a museum on the lower floors.

The remaining forty-five acres of the property, which had been deer park and groves, were held by Mr. Hoyt Sherman, an assignee of the Allen estate. On June 14, 1884, this entire acreage, except for seven acres retained by Benjamin Franklin Allen, was sold for $150,000, and the buyers were Hubbell and his partner, J.S.Polk. The firm of Hubbell and Polk, attorneys and brokers, speculated in land sales, organized stock companies, and built the city water works, as well as many of the large buildings in the city of Des Moines.

By mid-summer 1885, Weidenmann was revising the landscape at "Terrace Hill," altering the front lawn planting to afford better views of the mansion from Greenwood Avenue. He was also taking necessary data to revise other parts of the grounds. By December of

Terrace Hill, Des Moines, Iowa.

that year, he had prepared a plan for sub-dividing the thirty-eight acres that remained of the original estate, and shortly afterwards he completed the road drainage plans. Weidenmann took his site data back to his New York office to prepare these plans, and he collaborated with Mr. Pelton, the city surveyor for Des Moines, in staking out the plans on the ground for construction.

Weidenmann's plan consisted of a loop-road around "Terrace Hill" off of Greenwood Avenue. He also designed two other entrance roads to the tract off the Avenue, Greenwood Place and Westerly Avenue (now 28th Street). The eastern portion of the loop around the mansion was Terrace Road, and the western loop road was Allen Place, probably because Benjamin Franklin Allen had returned to Des Moines and built a three-story Gothic house along this road, slightly northwest of "Terrace Hill."

Forest drive meandered diagonally across the tract, and off it a secondary road, called Park Place because it eventually met Terrace Road which led to a large park planned for the south side of the tract. A railroad station was planned for the far end of the park, and a railroad track was to run across the rear boundary of the property. This railroad would carry the residents from their idyllic rural setting to the city for their daily work.

The roads throughout this residential park were to be planted with arching trees, and these, combined with the green lawns surrounding each house, would set the rural scene. Between the network of tree-lined, curving roads that sensitively followed the contours of the land were seventy-five house lots, averaging from one-half to three-quarter acres each.

While Weidenmann's plan was not followed in every detail, there is evidence that it was generally adhered to for laying out the lots. The park, railroad station, and the railroad track, however, were never built. The space designated as a park was sold for house lots.

It is interesting to compare this residential park with the Hill Park subdivision that Weidenmann did thirty years earlier on Staten Island. Both featured a rural ambience, where busy, city-working people could come home and relax in a private place situated on sweeping green lawns beneath arching shade trees. Every undulation of the terrain was respected, roads curving between and around them. Both projects had a large mansion with extensive grounds as their centerpieces. Where the projects differed was in the size of the building lots, the Hill Project featuring lots of several acres, while the Polk-Hubbell tract had lots of less than one acre.

The Iowa State Agricultural Society had recently acquired the Thornton farm, one-and-one-half miles east of the State Capitol in Des Moines. It was largely level land, some of it forested, with high bluffs rising at one side, which afforded vantage points for views towards the growing city.

The officers of the Agricultural Society, like Hubbell and Polk, knew that they had a good planning resource available to them. They asked Jacob Weidenmann to come and look at the site and offer planning suggestions. When Weidenmann saw the grounds he told the Society that "Nature has done every thing for the place which can possibly be desired, and if no mistake is made in the work to be done by art, Iowa will certainly have the finest fair grounds in the United States."

Much had to be included in the plan: a large main building for events and exhibits; a circular race track with adjacent viewing stands; many sheds and barns to house hogs, cattle, sheep, horses, poultry, hay and equipment; an amphitheater for events and performances; a large midway; and an extensive waterworks with forty-eight hydrants to serve all of the buildings, sixty-two dry-wells for discharged water, and an eight-thousand gallon water holding tank high on the bluff.

It is believed that Weidenmann did not draw a plan for this project. He actually withdrew from this one in the spring of 1886, leaving the rest of the work to a local architect, William F. Hackney. His reason for withdrawing from this commission is unknown, but perhaps he was only asked to present a broad concept to them later to be detailed by Hackney.

On September 3, 1886, after one-hundred-fifty men worked three months to build the structures and prepare the grounds, the fair opened with great fanfare; it was the 33rd annual exhibition, but none of the previous ones had been as large or complete as this. The grounds were beautifully laid out with a commodious midway down the center. On the left was the large, rail-enclosed race track with its long stands of bleachers along the midway side, and on the right of the midway were thirty livestock-exhibit buildings arranged in three, circular groups, the buildings arranged like the spokes of a wheel.

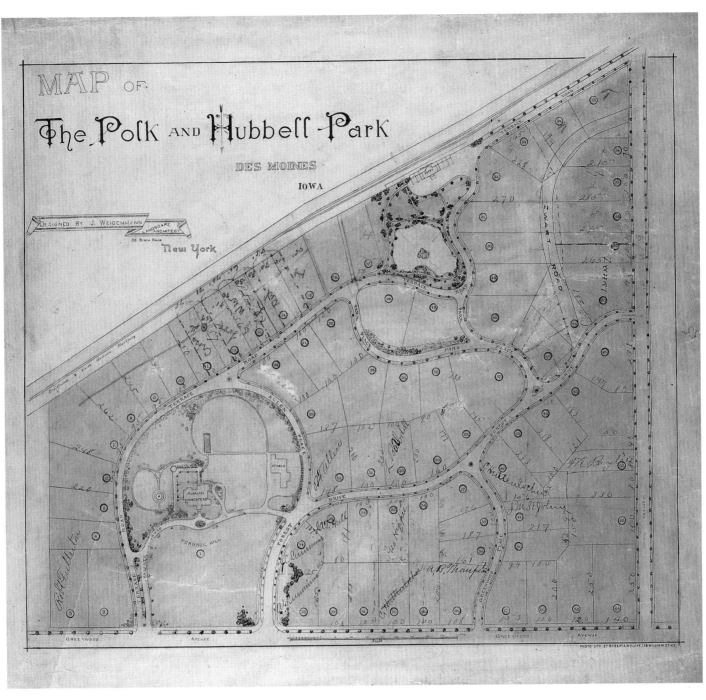

Weidenmann's site plan for the Polk-Hubbell Residential Park.

Beyond the racetrack at the base of the bluffs were other exhibit buildings, and part way up the bluff was the main building. An amphitheatre, built for outdoor events, utilized the slope for stepped seating. All of these varied elements were unified by a well-planned road system, and the roads were amply wide to handle the crowds and generously bordered with green lawn.

It is evident from a sketch that appeared in *The Iowa State Register* of August 29, 1886, that the fair grounds were carefully planned, and that the planner had integrated the natural features of the land with the requirements of a fair.

Jacob Weidenmann also consulted on plans for the grounds for the Iowa State Insane Asylum, but plans or accounts of his work have yet to be discovered. In a letter to Frederick Law Olmsted, during the winter of 1886, he wrote that though he had considerable work to do in the vicinity of New York, "I have more extensive work in Des Moines and Spirit Lake." Spirit Lake is one of the "Iowa Great Lakes," about 175 miles northwest of Des Moines just south of the Minnesota border. Today there is a town of Spirit Lake on the south shore of the lake by that name, and just south of the town is another lake, Lake East Okoboji that curves in a crescent to the south and west.

Research to date has not revealed what Weidenmann designed at Spirit Lake, but there was much going on there. For example, Justice Josiah Given of the Iowa Supreme Court was developing an area of cottages along the shore of West Okoboji Lake. Others were doing the same on Spirit Lake, and hotels and campgrounds were emerging everywhere. Most certainly, it was one of those projects that attracted Weidenmann.

Mount Hope Cemetery and Other Projects
Chicago, Illinois

Weidenmann's success with his various projects in Iowa, and his cordial acceptance by the people with whom he worked, encouraged him to think about moving his office to the Midwest. The long hours spent commuting between New York and Iowa usurped valuable creative time for which he was not being compensated. While Iowa was a rapidly growing state, his inclination was to locate in a more central place from which he could cover a wider region with shorter trips.

As he was contemplating this idea, he heard of a position that was available as planner and superintendent for a new cemetery that was projected for a large tract southwest of then central Chicago. He applied for the job, and was offered it because of his past experience in cemetery planning at Cedar Hill in Hartford.

In considering the move, however, he wrote to his friend Frederick Law Olmsted to seek his advice before taking this giant and costly step that would involve moving not only his office but also the entire family. Olmsted had been trying to convince him to apply for the position of Landscape Architect for Central Park in New York, but this position did not appeal to Weidenmann who responded that "I sincerely declare that I have neither the ambition nor the necessary qualifications for such a position nor would I accept the offer . . . under a management as the present one." Six months earlier, Olmsted had suggested that Weidenmann apply for the job as superintendent of the Park, but Weidenmann swept that suggestion aside by saying that he was not qualified for the job since he did not know enough about "practical gardening" to supervise workmen and carry out other details involved with the position. The fact was that he did not like some of the personalities involved with the Park and the politics they played.

Olmsted advised Weidenmann not to move to Chicago. We do not have Olmsted's letter to that effect, but we know that he advised against the move based on later comments made by Weidenmann. Olmsted knew the City of Chicago because he had drawn plans for the South Parks. He was also in constant correspondence with his friend, Horace William Shaler Cleveland (1814–1900), who had established an office in Chicago for the practice of landscape architecture in 1869. About the time Weidenmann was considering moving there in 1886, Cleveland was moving his office to Minneapolis where he would continue the work begun four years previously on the design of that city's park system.

Apparently, Cleveland and Olmsted had been discussing Weidenmann's proposed move and the status of landscape architecture, because in one of Cleveland's letters he wrote: "It is true enough that there is no appreciation of landscape gardening in Chicago — or in the West — and for that matter most of which passes for rural taste anywhere in the country is twaddle."

In early May of 1886, Weidenmann wrote to Olmsted thanking him profusely for his advice, but saying that he had decided to accept the Mount Hope offer so that he could have a steady job and not have to worry about the "fluctuations of business prosperity." He moved his family to Chicago in late May, though he had been commuting there since the previous autumn when he began his job.

Mr. William McCrea, president of the Mount Hope Board, and Mr. Rust, the vice-president, both of whom convinced him to take the position, were not there when he arrived to begin his work; McCrea was in California for nine months, and Rust was in Europe. Weidenmann was left to deal with the remainder of the Board, all land speculators interested in extracting as much income as possible from the 240 acre site they had put together.

Prior to Weidenmann's arrival in Chicago, Cleveland had drawn plans for a Catholic cemetery nearby and was asked to consult at Mount Hope. He advised the Board to have a topographic survey with cross-sections made of the site. With these data he could then draw a general plan that ". . . any engineer could put upon the ground." Cleveland informed them that he could not give up his work on the Minneapolis Park System to do any more than that. The Board decided to hire Weidenmann instead, who would not only draw the plans, but also become Superintendent of the Cemetery, and be allowed to take private commissions on his own time.

Cleveland tried to meet Weidenmann soon after he arrived in Chicago, but with his travels back and forth to Minneapolis, the preparations for his move there, and Weidenmann's getting started with the plans for Mount Hope, the two men were too busy, and as a consequence, they never met.

Weidenmann worked on the plans for Mount Hope over the winter, and they were ready for implementation by April. Mr. Rollins, a dry goods merchant and member of the Mount Hope Board, immediately stepped in and "assumed at once the right to dictate [to Weidenmann] in matters of an absolute professional character." Rollins was on the grounds every day from 7 a.m. until 5 p.m., giving orders and rearranging the plans according to his own taste and desires. Roads and paths were changed, as well as other features, greatly altering Weidenmann's plan and causing repeated struggles.

Feeling a sense of total frustration, Weidenmann asked for a meeting of the Board in an attempt to resolve this contentious situation. The Board responded with a meeting, but they didn't inform him or invite him to attend. At the meeting, Rollins presented a motion to cancel Weidenmann's contract for not following orders given by

Rollins, who represented the Cemetery Board, and for "not giving full attention to the interest of the cemetery." The motion carried.

Weidenmann had become friends with an elderly architect named Van Osdel, who advised him to bring suit upon the Mount Hope Cemetery Board, and to gather up all of the plans he had drawn for the Cemetery and retain them. This was done except for a watercolor rendering of the general plan that was in Rollins's possession. The day after the Board passed its motion to terminate Weidenmann's contract, an accidental fire destroyed all of the plans that were in possession of the Cemetery. The only ones remaining were Weidenmann's own and the rendering. The Board threatened a criminal suit against Weidenmann, but they were advised against it by their attorney. Instead they hired a Mr. Kern, a landscape gardener from St. Louis, to replace Weidenmann.

Within a few months after the Weidenmann family moved to Chicago, Jacob was without a job. Though they were situated in a comfortable house near the Lake, he had not had time to obtain any private commissions, and he feared that once word got around about his severance from Mount Hope, he might have difficulty securing any.

Again, his friend Olmsted came to the rescue with a letter of reference to the eminent architect William LeBaron Jenney, whom he knew because of Jenny's collaboration with Olmsted and Vaux on their Riverside, Illinois, residential park in the late 1860s. Jenny also practiced landscape architecture, though he is best known as the architect whose innovations—internal steel, or skeleton framing— led to the development of skyscrapers.

When the two met, Jenny suggested that Weidenmann apply for the job of superintendent of West Park, but it appears that Weidenmann decided against it, perhaps for the same reasons he didn't apply as park superintendent in New York. Jenney then used Weidenmann's talents to prepare an improvement plan for Mackinac Island, Michigan, where Jenney had a summer home. Weidenmann also developed the plans for remodeling the fourteen-acre Union Park in Chicago, working in his own home office, though the plans went out over both his and Jenney's signatures.

The Reverend Joseph Cummings, D.D., president of Northwestern University, engaged Weidenmann's services to draw a master plan for the forty-five acre campus in Evanston, along the shores of Lake Michigan, including the siting of new structures. Some substantial buildings had been constructed, and these were to be incorporated into the new plan, along with and an entire road and drainage system. Weidenmann worked with the natural landscape, as usual, carefully protecting the groves of "handsome oaks."

It took almost two years for the Weidenmann vs. Mount Hope Cemetery suit to go to trial in the Superior Court. Weidenmann was advised to hire top-notch criminal lawyers, which he did in the name of Thomas B. Bryan and Robert Hervey. Key witnesses were named, and Olmsted was able to give his deposition in Brookline for presentation at the trial by the attorneys. The case finally came forward on March 12, 1888, but it was again postponed until April 23rd.

Several witnesses were heard on Weidenmann's behalf. One of them was Mr. George Moore, President of the Board at Cedar Hill Cemetery in Hartford. Mount Hope's attorney alleged that on a trip East, Mr. Kern, the new superintendent of the Mount Hope Cemetery, discovered that Weidenmann had been disgracefully discharged as superintendent of Cedar Hill because of his inability and extravagance, and that he then took flight to Europe after having embezzled various sums of money. George Moore was so indignant about these accusations that he required that Kern pay fifty dollars just to examine the Cedar Hill records when he came to Hartford, and at the trial he defended Weidenmann, firmly refuting all charges.

Olmsted's own deposition was then presented. It began by going back to when they first worked together professionally in 1862, executing the plans for the grounds at the Hartford Retreat for the Insane, and continued through all of their collaborations to the day of the trial. Olmsted also devoted a good part of his deposition to explaining how well qualified Weidenmann was by virtue of his formal education and also his professional practice of over thirty years, which he described in infinite detail. A good portion of his deposition dealt with how a professional landscape architect should function, and concluded that Weidenmann had performed accordingly.

Testifying also in Weidenmann's behalf was Peter A. Dey of Des Moines, who spoke of Weidenmann's exemplary plans for the Polk-Hubbell residential park, and the State Capitol project, describing their detail and accuracy. Then Reverend Joseph Cummings, praised Weidenmann's "ability and good taste" in draw-ing the master plan for Northwestern University, and William

LeBaron Jenney also came to his defense with good words about their collaboration on Union Park in Chicago, and Mackinac Island in Michigan. Seven major witnesses testified in Weidenmann's behalf.

There was a long waiting period before Judge Gary rendered his decision on July 11, 1888. He decreed that Mount Hope Cemetery was required to pay the full amount of Weidenmann's five-year contract, or $17,500.00, minus the $2,800 he had already been paid. Before this day of judgment, Mount Hope had dropped all of its charges except one—Weidenmann's alleged disobedience towards members of the Board.

The judge, in rendering his decision, stated that the Board had no right to interfere with the "minor details of Weidenmann's management after they approved the plans and appointed him superintendent to execute the same." He used, as an example, his hiring a cabinetmaker, and after telling him what wood and trimming he would use, he would have no right to tell him which tools to use to perform the work. He further added that interfering with the employee's work, and then dismissing him for disobedience, was a breach of contract.

In the interim, before the judge's decision was rendered, Weidenmann decided to leave Chicago and return to New York. He wrote to Olmsted saying, "I am confident of winning the suit and so are my lawyers, of course, but in spite of this, the nearest future troubles me very much for I can't stay here, and it seems to me that the only thing left is to return to New York and commence new again at the age of 59."

Several times Weidenmann wrote to Olmsted saying that he should have heeded his advice not to take the job and settle in Chicago, and on September 11, he wrote again saying, "for nearly thirty years that I have enjoyed the opportunity of your acquaintance, I feel that although far below your position, you always acted as a friend. This friendship, so liberally accorded, has been a source of greatest satisfaction to me. I feel it more than ever before and sincerely hope it will continue in spite of many mistakes and misunderstandings on my part."

Chapter Seven

"American Garden Architecture" and "Modern Cemeteries"

With the success of his book *Beautifying Country Homes,* Weidenmann had begun thinking about another project for educating the public about his chosen field of landscape architecture. It was a way to fill open time between commissions, and something he could do at home in the evenings and on weekends. Perhaps he could also earn an extra dollar or two as reserve for when the economy was on a downswing.

The plans, sketches, and drawings in his office had begun to accumulate as they do for all designers. Why not organize these and publish them for sale, he thought? Doing so would fulfill a twofold purpose: the public could learn from them, and at the same time, he would be advertising his profession. For this work, he engaged the engraver W. G. Phillips to make the necessary plates for printing.

Weidenmann organized his drawings into twelve sections of five plates each. Each plate would be printed on a large sheet of 12 by 20 inches. There would be a paper cover protecting the drawings, and inside the front cover would be brief explanations of a paragraph or two for each plan included. Inside the rear cover, an index detailing the entire twelve sections of the series would appear.

Each section would be published monthly and sell for one-dollar-fifty-cents per monthly issue, or twelve dollars for a year's subscription. In appearance, the monthly editions were quite like a magazine, or journal, of folio size. Frederick Kost of New York City was the printer, and the first edition went on sale in January 1877.

The first issue, as would all of the projected issues, contained six plates. The first was of a gate for the estate of Colonel Sweeting Miles (which has been described in Chapter Five). Plates 2 and 3 showed Charles Brainard's grapery in Hartford, one a perspective of the entire glass-domed grapery, and the other a cross-section and a floor plan. For variety, Weidenmann prepared Plate 4 as a set of two plans for garden terraces, the top being for Charles Dana's estate in Oyster Bay, and the other for Henry B. Hyde's "Masquetux," (both estates described and pictured earlier in Chapter Five).

The final two plates in this first edition are perspective views: plan, and elevation for the lodge and gatehouse that Weidenmann designed for the Asylum for the Insane in Concord, New Hampshire. These are the same drawings that he recommended as an entrance for Cedar Hill Cemetery, in Hartford, for which he suggested removing the bell tower (see Cedar Hill Cemetery, Chapter Two).

The index inside the rear cover indicates that each of the monthly

Cover for
first issue
of *American
Garden
Architecture.*

folios would contain a mixture of projects ranging from barns, poultry houses, boat houses, and various kinds of pavilions in some, to gates, ice houses, garden seats, bridges, and windmills in others. Bowling alleys, fountains, green houses, arbors, and water storage towers would be the subjects for other issues. Three of the series would focus on one project each: a cottage park, kiosks, and aviaries.

As mentioned, the first number was released in January 1877. While the plates were engraved for most of the subsequent editions, there is no evidence that they were ever printed. There is much speculation concerning why the series failed. Some suggest that with the emergence of several complete, hard covered books on landscape gardening, this large, soft-covered folio comprising only six drawings, hard to read in an easy-chair or in bed, had limited appeal. Others suggest that during hard economic times, the price was high when one could purchase an entire book on landscape gardening for just a few dollars.

Weidenmann might have done better by publishing all seventy-two of the projected engravings in one or two hard-covered compendiums, adding more complete texts describing each, much as he did for his *Beautifying Country Homes*. Such a publication might have had broader appeal at least for the wealthy, especially those who had been his clients, and their friends.

This unsuccessful attempt did not impede Weidenmann's writing efforts. Apparently he had been collecting material on rural cemeteries to add to his own Cedar Hill experience, both as its designer and superintendent. Given this background, he decided to write a two-part article, the first being on a new concept for cemetery design to replace established ideas that were no longer effective in growing cities. The second part detailed certain principles to consider in developing the new cemetery plan. These appeared in tandem the last two weeks of September, 1881, in *The American Architect and Building News*, a weekly journal.

The 17 September piece began by acknowledging the book *God's Acre Beautiful*, a popular work written by the eminent English horticulturist, William Robinson (1838–1935), also founder and editor of the flourishing weekly paper, *The Garden*, as well as its sister monthly called *Gardening Illustrated*. Weidenmann referred the reader to a section in Robinson's book that discussed the "horrors" of over-crowded burial places in large cities. He then advocated a reformation whereby new burial places would be centralized in large tracts, not scattered throughout cities in small plots promoted by land speculators desiring to sell many lots at high prices. Another aspect of the reformation process would be to use land within new cemeteries economically, with only thirty square feet devoted to each grave instead of larger spaces required to accommodate huge monuments or other ornaments; obviously, he was not referring to spacious rural cemeteries. As a final step in the reformation process Weidenmann suggested drastically revising interment practices.

Related to the economic and careful use of burial space, Weidenmann emphasized that, by not using above-ground monuments, in a hundred years or more after the burial, the plots could be recycled, and certainly grave sites reserved for family members that were not used could be resold.

Part Two of the article appeared in the September 24, 1881 issue of *The American Architect and Building News*. Mausolea were recommended as a way to concentrate family burials, providing an efficient and impressive feature in an expanse of open lawn, or surrounded by graves with ground-flush markers rather than upright monuments. As mentioned previously, Weidenmann was a strong advocate of marking graves in this manner not only to preserve large expanses of lawn without visual interruptions, but also because in future years, areas with flush markers could be recycled since they would not have large, permanently set monuments.

He wrote in detail about a system for marking the locations of coffins underground by encircling them with a four-inch layer of white sand. The sand would stay white over the centuries, even while in contact with dark soil and the decomposition of the corpse and coffin would not alter the sand's color. By so marking each burial, he maintained, one of the horrors of over-crowded burial spaces would be avoided, especially during the recycling process, because the gravedigger would readily see where a former burial had taken place. Of course, Weidenman was not in favor of burial vaults because they would cause permanent obstructions.

In the final section of this article, Weidenmann discussed new devices in use in Europe to assist with the interment, and suggested using them here to make the process simpler. These would help to lower the casket into the grave, instead of having several men awkwardly let it down. Devices were also available for refilling the grave in a manner avoiding the slow, agonizing, shovelful-by-shovelful process then in use, a painful and "provoking scene" for the bereaved family.

Proposed arrangement for summer cottages.
From *American Garden Architecture*.

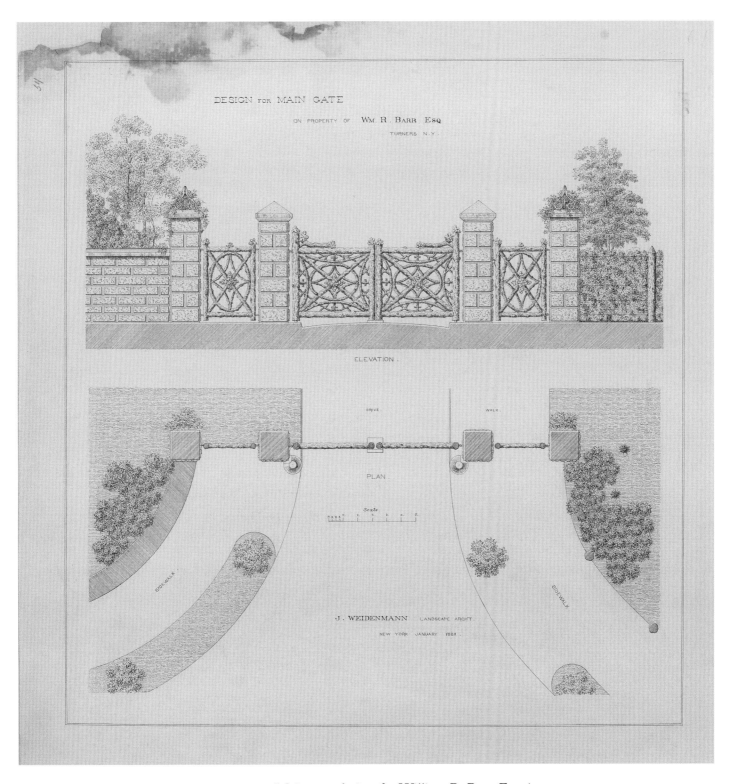

Main gate design for William R. Barr, Esquire,
From *American Garden Architecture*.

Sketch for a flush grave marker.
From *Modern Cemeteries*.

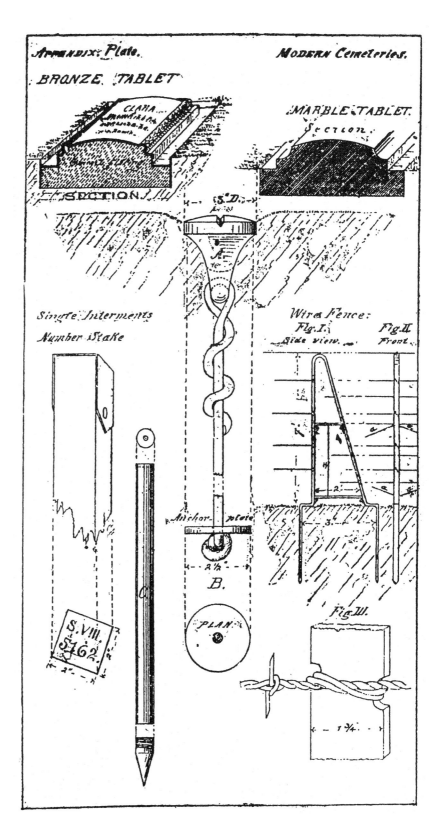

The success of this two-part article gave Weidenmann the idea to write a long essay on cemetery planning and management. In reality, his many commissions in the early 1880s, including travel back and forth to Iowa, did not leave many hours for writing. He was not able to complete his long essay, which he called *Modern Cemeteries,* until later in the decade, during the nineteen-month period when he was waiting for his Mount Hope Cemetery trial and did not have many other commissions. At that time he wrote to his friend Olmsted:

> Presently I occupy my vast leisure time writing my essay on "Modern Cemeteries" which commenced to appear in *The Building Budget,* an architecture journal published in the City [Chicago] by H. Lord Gay who agrees to publish it in book form (about 200 pages) with illustrations, plans, and diagrams, and so you see my destiny is to work for the grave diggers.

He did complete the work, a long, detailed essay, which in print consisted of 113 pages. It begins with a brief history of burials, quickly evolving into an explanation of the rural cemetery movement which began at Mount Auburn Cemetery, in Cambridge, Massachusetts (1831), and quickly spread to Laurel Hill Cemetery in Philadelphia (1835), Greenwood Cemetery in Brooklyn, New York (1838), and afterwards expanded rapidly throughout the country. As Weidenmann wrote about the concept, he recalled at length the introduction of the open lawn system to Spring Grove Cemetery in Cincinnati by his friend, Adolph Strauch.

The essay continued with an explanation of the planning process, and the selection of cemetery sites that have suitable soil types, and are in good locations with relation to the city they will serve. The importance of natural features, such as water, rolling terrain, and views was stressed. Foresight in planning for future expansion, and buffering the cemetery from encroaching neighbors were also noted as part of the planning process.

Throughout the essay, Weidenmann used actual cemeteries as case examples, and he especially relied on his experiences at Cedar Hill. He told about a section of the cemetery where the Board had hoped to sell prime lots because of its location high on a ridge that had fine views, but as the section was carefully investigated, bedrock was found close to the surface. The problem was solved by quarrying out the rock to use as a firm base for the roads being built, and then using the soil cut from the road base to fill in the quarried section.

The importance of hiring a landscape architect to draw the plans was stressed, and then Weidenmann explained the types of plans that the landscape architect should provide: the general plan, road and drainage plans, section plans, planting plans, and lot layout plans for each burial section. He stressed that the open lawn system should be basic to all these plans.

Lot layout, the primary focus for a cemetery, follows this basic planning section. Here he discussed the details of interments, from individual and family lots, to society burial lots, where members of a group, club, or organization may wish to be buried together.

Related to burials and the sale of lots of whatever type, the sales system and method of recording were emphasized, and their long-range importance was stressed in detail. Following these chapters on basic and detailed planning, Weidenmann wisely covered the whole matter of cemetery maintenance and its importance not only for upkeep, but also to set a peaceful and serene ambience for memorializing the dead.

While the landscape is basic to a cemetery, Weidenmann also stressed the place of architecture as part of this landscape. Various examples, or sketches, of receiving vaults and mausolea are shown, and each type is carefully described. Presented are free-standing mausolea, as well as vaults and mausolea built into hillsides. The text which follows presents the advantages and disadvantages of each type.

The final chapter of the essay was entitled "The Cemetery of the Future," actually a summary of the entire piece. Not surprisingly, Weidenmann reiterated the importance of the open lawn concept, where preferably no upright monuments, fences, or flowers planted in the ground would be allowed, but where natural landscape elements—water, trees, shrubs, views and vistas—are featured. As a final note, he stressed that in the future, the use of burial urns for cremations would have to be considered as space, especially in cities, becomes scarce.

Weidenmann and Mr. H. Lord Gay, publisher of *The Building Budget*, signed a contract to print the essay in book form; however, Gay soon fell into financial hardship and the whole process ceased, the contract broken. Again, Weidenmann wrote to his friend Olmsted saying:

> I have been unfortunate in everything in Chicago. The publisher agreed by contract to get out everything in book form in first class style three months after the manuscript

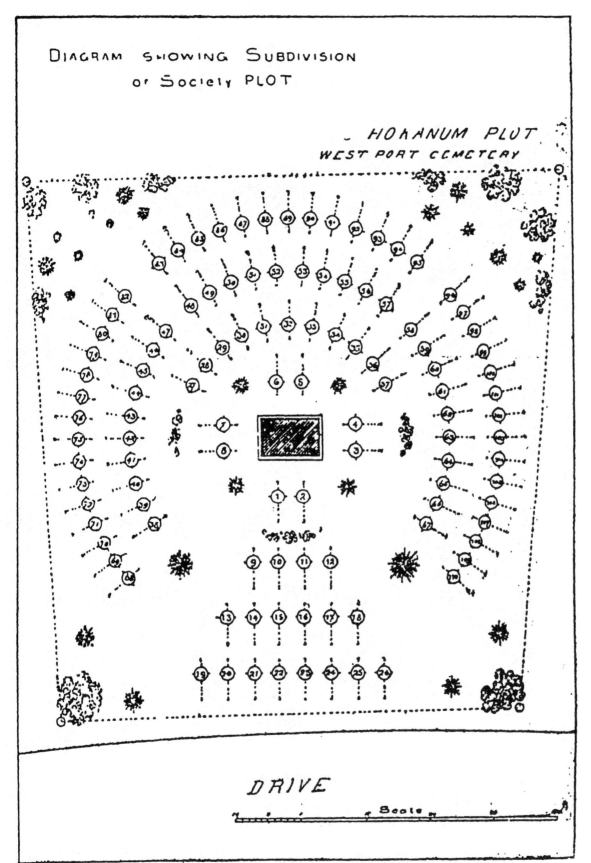

DIAGRAM SHOWING SUBDIVISION
OF SOCIETY PLOT

HOKANUM PLOT
WEST PORT CEMETERY

DRIVE

Scale

Plan for a society
burial plot. From
Modern Cemeteries.

would be printed in *The Building Budget,* but when I pointed to the contract 12 months later, Mr. Gay declared that he was financially broken and could do nothing more [than] turn the electroplates over to me, as they left the press of *The Budget,* with 400 copies printed in loose sheets.

Weidenmann was able to turn the printed pages over to *The Monumental News,* a monthly journal "devoted to cemetery news," making a few revisions by adding some of the illustrations that had been omitted from the serial essay. It was printed with "a cheap paper cover" in 1888. Proceeds from the sale of *Modern Cemeteries* went to pay for the limited printing.

Few copies of *Modern Cemeteries* survive, in part because of the small number produced, but also because the pages and cover were printed on cheap, high acid paper, which caused them to deteriorate rapidly. This is unfortunate, because *Modern Cemeteries* was an excellent guide for cemetery planning and management, with forward-thinking concepts that still apply to cemetery planning well over a century later.

PLAN of CRYPT.

Scheme for one type of mausoleum. From *Modern Cemeteries*.

Chapter Eight

New York: "Commencing New"

The Weidenmanns arranged to rent a house at 195 Sixth Avenue in Brooklyn, a few blocks from Prospect Park. Jacob probably made an advance trip to find the place and also to search for an office location. In the interim, between this arrangement and the family's arrival in Brooklyn, the place had been let to someone else. Fortunately, the Weidenmanns were able to find an apartment even closer to the Park, at 123 Berkeley Place. Being near Prospect Park seemed to be important to the family despite the fact that it was not being managed according to the original Olmsted and Vaux design, and massive alterations were taking place, not for the better.

For an office location, Weidenmann found space in the Metropolitan Savings Bank Building, and for the remainder of his career his address was 1 Third Avenue, "at the corner of Third and Seventh, opposite Cooper Union," as his announcement stated. He had arranged to rent this office prior to his return to the City with his family during the third week of October, 1888.

Easing into his new practice was a slow process because he had to become known again after an absence of several years. Certainly his list of credentials was extensive: all of his early work in Hartford, the Long Island estates including his prize-winning "Masquetux," his consultation and work at the Hot Springs Reservation in Arkansas, the work at the Iowa State Capitol, and his numerous residential sub-divisions starting with Staten Island, then Long Island, and Des Moines. He printed an announcement heralding his practice and credentials, including his expertise in cemetery design.

His announcement also listed his fees for various types of consultations. He charged five dollars per acre for general sub-division plans, but for detailed plans for roads, drainage, etc., twenty dollars per acre. If the site was less than ten acres, the fee would range from thirty to one hundred dollars per acre, depending upon the complexity of the project. Charges for travel expenses were added as extras.

Soon the commissions flowed into his office. He was asked to advise on a plan for the grounds at Brooklyn College, and also for Calvary Church, and St. Patrick Cemetery. Of these commissions we have no details, only his daughter's report and two of his letters merely naming the projects. It is almost certain that he hoped to be asked to consult on Prospect Park in Brooklyn, but eventually he decided that the politics there and the arrogance of the management precluded any such arrangement.

Weidenmann began commuting to Iowa again in 1890. The Executive Council for the Improvements of the State Capitol Grounds was ready to build the Grand Stair Plaza after a four-year hiatus. Because construction of the Plaza was not part of the initial phase, he had prepared only the general plan for this Plaza, and had been requested to withhold the construction details until later. After some minor adjustments to his schedule of charges, he was called back to Des Moines, arriving on November 18, 1890. He spent most of this visit gathering final measurements and other details necessary for completing the plans. Fortunately for Weidenmann, the Council also appointed General Edward Wright to act as superintendent in charge of the work when construction actually began, and after Wright's resignation, Mr. C.W. Crellin replaced him. These appointments were helpful to Weidenmann, resulting in fewer trips to Des Moines.

During the early winter he worked diligently on the plans and by February 6, 1891, he was back in Iowa to present them, along with a ten page explanatory report, this being one of the first typewritten documents emanating from his office. The Council asked him also to prepare final drainage, gas lighting, and water supply plans, and to design candelabras (lamps) for illuminating the grounds. As part of his design package he also prepared a large perspective drawing, rendered in water color, which he used to illustrate his oral presentation.

At the bottom of the Grand Stair Plaza Weidenmann designed a "Centre Pier" intended to be the focal point upon arrival. It would have a drinking fountain for man and beast at its base, and a statue on top, both of these features facing Ninth Street. The dimensions of the base of the Pier were given as sixteen by twenty-six feet and eight inches and it would be five-feet-six- inches high. The pier would be faced with granite flags six inches thick. The basin of the drinking fountain, inserted into the base, was also of granite with a polished rim. The fountain's niche was recessed six inches, and within it a lion's head encircled the water jet that sprayed water into the basin below.

Upon this base, or plinth, a large pedestal of granite was proposed, and on it a statue, either sculpted of marble or cast in bronze, would be placed. Weidenmann stated in his report that the reason for having this pier, as well as a second one adjacent to the first terrace, called the Fountain Terrace, was to break up the forty foot wide expanse of steps, and also to "relieve the eye at the approach from Locust Street of an otherwise monotonous character."

The second Pier, between the Fountain and Grand Terraces, would have sunken panels on its face upon which memorials could be affixed. The top of this Pier would contain a large planter in which low-spreading annuals would grow, and he cited portulacas as a possibility because they would withstand the dry heat of summer. This planter was complemented by two semi-circular planters on either end of the uppermost, or Grand Terrace.

The Grand Terrace had an exedra, or curved stone seat, at each end. The granite for these was to be roughly axed, patent hammered, or chiseled, in order to eliminate a smooth surface that would invite vandalism. Mention was made of the high elevation of the Terrace, one hundred feet above the Des Moines River, affording a pleasing view for all visitors. The two semi-circular flowerbeds mentioned above were planned for the center of the circle formed by the exedras, and these would be planted with annuals to be changed with the seasons. These flower beds, along with the large planter atop the Pier in the center of this Terrace's west side, were intended for "picturesque effect in producing the needed contrast by their gay colors and pleasing foliage." From this Grand Terrace, a long flight of steps led to the Capitol front. The center of this Terrace was left open, free of any ornamental features, so that receptions and "public assemblages" could be held, using the steps as seats, much like an amphitheatre.

Having addressed the basic plan details, Weidenmann made specific suggestions for the ornamental features to embellish the Stair Plaza. For the statue to adorn the Pier at the entrance he suggested "The Pioneer Group of the Former Territory," a father, son, and their Native American guide, looking for a place to settle. The artist selected was Karl Gerhardt, of Hartford, Connecticut, a machinist turned sculptor, who had attained some renown for his sculptures of Ulysses S. Grant and Samuel Clemens (Mark Twain), as well as several other well-known people. He had received much of his training through the sponsorship of Clemens who also funded his years of study in Paris under the famous sculptor Francois Jouffroy, who had previously instructed Augustus St. Gaudens. Gerhardt was paid $4,500.00 for this statue (about $94,500.00 today).

As mentioned previously, Weidenmann had recommended a tradi-

Jacob Weidenmann's rendering for half of the symmetrical
Grand Stair Plaza, Iowa State Capitol, Des Moines.

tional lion's head for the jet surround in the drinking fountain situated in the base of the statue; however, the Council felt that it would be more appropriate to have a buffalo's head instead. The following note appeared in the *Iowa State Register* on November 18, 1891:

> The Executive Council, at its meeting yesterday, made a small alteration in the plans of the Capitol Improvements. It will not be the mouth of a lion from out which the water shall flow at the drinking fountain at the foot of the main esplanade, as has been announced, but a buffalo's. This change is a tribute to the sentimentalism which bewails the loss of the animal of the prairie and seeks to perpetuate his fame.

The buffalo head, indeed a welcome change, was sculpted by the New York artist Alexander Doyle for $500.00. Doyle also made the bronze tablet of the Great Seal of Iowa that is set in the recess of the second Grand Pier between the Fountain and Grand terraces. His fee for this work was $650.00.

Weidenmann's written report was quite specific that a fountain be placed in the center of the first large terrace, called the Fountain Terrace, just above the first Grand Pier and statue. It would sit in the center of a twenty-six foot diameter pool. He wrote that the fountain would be "the most attractive feature of the Capitol grounds" and, therefore, must receive the Council's full attention.

The fountain pool was to be cast concrete, with an eighteen-inch-high rim of grey granite, and polished, convex granite coping would cap this rim, topped with an ornamental railing of bronze. The fountain itself would consist of a large urn in the center from which water overflowed, the urn being set on a granite pedestal within which the water and overflow pipes would be concealed, with the overflow connecting to the city sewer. Weidenman specified that the correct urn for this project could be purchased from the J. L. Mott Company, catalogue number 11–13L.

The Council did not follow Weidenmann's suggestion for the fountain design. To save money, they had the Scoville Plumbing Company of Des Moines, install a cheaper cast iron fountain, and the American Brass and Metal Works of Detroit provided the railing. The fountain purchased had a maiden at the top, holding an urn of flowing water that cascaded into a series of three basins that increased in size from top to bottom, the water finally tumbling into the pool below. This was a common fountain design that was available from any number of foundries dealing in cast iron.

Over the years, the fountain fell into disrepair. Since its design was supposedly a copy of one that had been displayed at the 1876 Centennial Exhibition in Philadelphia, one hundred years later, when the 1976 Bicentennial celebrations occurred, the fountain was replaced, but not with an exact replica. Unfortunately, the present fountain, unlike the earlier one, is out of scale with the large Fountain Terrace.

On August 30, 1892, *The Iowa State Register* reported:
> The capitol grounds area is a thing of beauty, in marked contrast with a year ago, when the surroundings of the great building were a mass of rugged earth and ugly debris. The thousands of people who will visit it during fair time will not only look through the structure with pride, but upon the green sward and choice flowers surrounding with admiration. There is no more lovely view anywhere than the west portico of the building, comprehending at a glance the main part of the capitol lawn and the greater part of the city.

During the last century, changes were made to the landscape. Monuments stand where the circular flowerbeds were in the exedras of the Grand Terrace. In 1913, the grounds were greatly expanded according to a plan drawn by E. L. Madqueray in which the Capitol campus spread from a single block to thirty-one acres. During this transformation, much of Weidenmann's original planting scheme was revised, but his Stair Plaza, with only the few revisions mentioned above, remains as he designed it. Along with Bushnell Park and Cedar Hill Cemetery in Hartford, this Capitol project stands as a lasting memorial to his finer work. Weidenmann himself considered the Iowa Capitol project "the most detailed work I ever prepared."

Residential Subdivision and Park for Colonel Alexander Pope
Hartford, Connecticut

Colonel Albert Pope, a veteran of the Civil War, started the Pope Manufacturing Company in Hartford in 1877 for the production of bicycles. He had seen his first two-wheeled vehicle at the Centennial Exposition in Philadelphia in 1876, and this inspired him to look into the possibility of bringing these sleek contraptions to Hartford. His research was successful, and soon he was able to start manufacturing several models of "Columbia Cycles," these popular "wheels" selling by the thousands. His production methods, employing precision machining and interchangeable parts laid the groundwork for the mass production of automobiles, which would soon follow.

"The Pioneer of the Former Territory," by Karl Gerhardt, Grand
Stair Plaza, Iowa State Capitol, with the watering fountain below.
Note the Fountain Terrace above.

Buffalo head watering fountain, and the Iowa State Seal,
by Alexander Doyle. Grand Stair Plaza, Iowa State Capitol.

Pope owned considerable real estate not far from his factory. He had been in contact with architect George Keller about building a large residential subdivision on a portion of these ninety acres. Keller, whom the reader will recall was the architect of the Soldiers and Sailors Memorial Arch in Bushnell Park, suggested that his friend Jacob Weidenmann be asked to lay out the general plan. When he met with Colonel Pope, Weidenmann was also asked to design a park between the Park River and Pope's factory property. A long drive had been constructed on one side of the parcel, which led to the new Trinity College campus. Weidenmann soon learned that the Olmsted Office had been contacted to design a park on the "Quarry Tract," probably the site of the present Rocky Ridge Park on the western edge of the Trinity College campus.

Weidenmann completed the preliminary plans for these two projects after several trips to Hartford to confer with Colonel Pope, George Keller, and others. These meetings took place late in 1892, but by early 1893, Weidenmann was aware that his health was declining. He would never be able to advance his schematic plans to final drawings.

In January 1893, Jacob Weidenmann began suffering from "remittent fever" during the time he was working on plans for the Pope project. In the third week of January he was in such a weakened state that he could not leave his bed in the second floor apartment at 123 Berkeley Place. Two weeks afterwards, on February 6, 1893, at three o'clock in the afternoon, he died of complications caused by acute nephritis, or kidney disease. He was sixty-three years old.

His body was held at Greenwood Cemetery, Brooklyn, until May 9 when it was transported to Cedar Hill Cemetery in Hartford for burial in Lot 3, section 7, near the ornamental foreground that he so ingeniously designed. It is presumed that the Cemetery Board presented the Weidenmann family with this lot. His wife and three daughters were later buried by his side.

During Weidenmann's final illness, Colonel Pope decided not to proceed with his residential subdivision. Instead, he chose to create a public park of the entire ninety acres because he believed that "the success of any manufacturing enterprise depends on the health, happiness, and orderly life of its employees." With this idea in mind, Pope hired the Olmsted Firm to make plans for Pope Park. They were completed in 1898, and during the planning period the tract was deeded to the City of Hartford.

During the period when the Olmsteds were planning Pope Park (1895–1898), George Keller was designing houses to be built on Columbia Street and Park Terrace, which bordered the Park on the southeast side. Keller saved 24 Park Row to build a house for himself and his family.

Another commission that ran concurrently with Colonel Pope's and one that was also never completed because of Weidenmann's death was a plan for the estate of Mr. Solomon Loeb, in the coastal resort town of Sea Bright, New Jersey. Loeb was the founder of the banking house of Kuhn, Loeb, and Company in New York City.

Concerns of the Profession and Weidenmann's Contributions

In the second half of the nineteenth century, the field of landscape architecture was emerging as we know it today. The "pioneers" who cast the model for the profession were Frederick Law Olmsted and Calvert Vaux, Horace William Shaler Cleveland, and Jacob Weidenmann.

These four practitioners believed strongly that all landscape planning should be based on a careful analysis of the natural landscape on any site, and that a landscape plan proposed, for whatever purpose, should respect the landscape that nature provided. Elements, such as ledges and rocks, ground formations, views and vistas, lakes, ponds and streams, and trees and shrubs, should be respected and utilized in the planned landscape. While these early landscape architects practiced what they preached, as did subsequent professionals, many who were posing as landscape architects did not. Today, especially after the publication of Ian L. McHarg's "Design with Nature" in 1967, the concept of designing with nature has become basic to all licensed landscape architects.

These early "pioneers" were aware of problems concerning the public's perception of landscape architecture, and also their lack of understanding of the need for preserving the natural, or best of all landscapes. Also, there were too many individuals entering the field, posing as professionals, who had no real understanding of the broad picture. They satisfied their unknowing clientele by creating pretty, gaudy, flower gardens, and adding bold statues and other ornaments to the landscape, focusing on petty details while ignoring the broader natural picture.

The handful of qualified landscape architects practicing in the second half of the nineteenth century constantly commiserated with one another in letters and when they met. The correspondence between Cleveland and Olmsted was filled with these laments. Cleveland wrote that he had drawn a plan for one client who owned a dramatic mountainous site, full of breath taking views, and how he planned the landscape so that these views would be featured from every vantage point. When his client received the plans, he wrote back saying that he was " . . . disappointed that I indicated no provision for statues, vases [urns], or rustic ornaments, and made no paths except where actually necessary." As a parting comment, though, the client did add that, in general, he was pleased with the basic plan.

In another letter Cleveland complained about a person he met who had seen the landscape he had designed for Drexel Boulevard in Chicago. What the person liked about it was a carpet bed of flowers, added by someone else, probably the gardener, that represented three men in a boat, "all done to perfection with different colored plants and flowers." Another landscape architect referred to this type of carpet bedding as "Pimples on the Face of Nature," the title of an article he wrote for a popular magazine.

Cleveland went on to say that he felt two types of parks were needed, one for "the comparatively few who need seclusion and the beauty of nature," and the other for the "multitude who can only enjoy solitude in a crowd to whom any work is artistic in proportion as it is artificial, and who unfortunately exert the controlling influence in almost every community." He went on to say that he wished that a crusade could be launched against the fashionable desecration of every scene of wild natural beauty.

Another point that troubled these nineteenth century landscape architects was, as mentioned previously, people who served on decision making committees or boards, who thought themselves competent enough to drastically alter recommendations made by the professionals. Olmsted made a big point of this during his deposition for Weidenmann's Mount Hope Cemetery trial by saying:

> When I am employed professionally, I do not serve under the direction of anyone. My business is to give advice in the form of . . . drawings and plans . . . and to see them executed.

Another landscape architect at the same time referred to the "hindrances imposed by park commissioners and politicians" as "gravel in the cog-wheels."

They all complained about the incompetent practitioners who were posing as landscape architects, and Weidenmann wrote that it was much regretted that "this art profession, too well known and yet too little understood, is tossed like a football by florists, gardeners, and nurserymen, by engineers, architects, and surveyors, whoever gets a chance to practice, criticize, slur, or slander, publicly or directly." The legitimate landscape architects considered it important to educate the public regarding what the field of landscape architecture really was, and the importance of hiring bona fide professionals to advise. All of their concerns eventually led to licensing laws, but one hundred years later.

Weidenmann asserted that there were two major ways to correct these problems. One was to educate the public that landscape architecture was about arranging a workable landscape gracefully, harmoniously, and economically on the natural landscape. He strove assiduously towards this end, and was one of the first landscape architects wanting to educate the public on good landscape planning, which he did in the books he published and through his journal articles. He believed that it was the duty of a landscape architect to impart his knowledge through writing, a difficult task for many practitioners to perform to this day. Graphic expression is quite different from written expression, and many landscape architects have difficulty practicing both tasks simultaneously. Also, when times are good and design projects are plentiful, it is hard to find time to write.

This is a problem that exists within the profession to this day. As this book is being written, in the June 2006 issue of *Landscape Architecture,* the monthly journal of the American Society of Landscape Architects, there is an article on "the dearth of critical writing" amongst landscape architects. Weidenmann, well disciplined as he was, not only had the aptitude, but also found time to write as well as design.

He also was an ardent believer in the need for schools of landscape architecture with a prescribed curriculum for training young people in a standardized manner. He hoped that if the first school spawned other schools, this standardized curriculum would be followed. He suggested a four-year curriculum where all aspects of the profession would be taught, beginning with a multitude of courses in design, followed by others in graphics, sketching, drawing, and modeling. Then there would be courses dealing with the land: soils, grading, contouring, drainage, and road design. Other courses would teach architecture and structural design. Not to be overlooked would be the courses in botany and plant materials.

The curriculum that Weidenmann proposed is strikingly similar to what is taught in accredited programs of landscape architecture today, except that one hundred years ago he could not foresee the age of computers. He was the only landscape architect practicing in America in the nineteenth century who had the benefit of college training in most of the fields that he prescribed, though he had to compose his own curriculum by taking courses at various institutions. Most other landscape architects, such as Olmsted, Cleveland, Copeland, and others, were self-trained by reading, travel, and varied practical experience. That was the only way a person could learn the profession then.

Weidenmann actually took apprentices to train as landscape architects. They were accepted on a trial basis for three weeks, and if he found them satisfactory "to warrant [them] the acquisition of our profession," the apprentice would then sign an agreement to serve for three years for which he would be paid one hundred dollars the first year, two hundred the second, and three hundred for the third.

While taking on apprentices was his own way of training people to be competent landscape architects, he saw this as an inadequate system. Whenever he could, he would promote the establishment of standardized landscape architecture schools, or schools that would offer a curriculum accepted by the profession. He felt so strongly about this matter that when Professor Charles Sargent founded the weekly journal called *Garden and Forest* in 1889, which carried articles on landscape architecture in practically every issue, Weidenmann wrote to John Charles Olmsted, his friend's son, saying that he wished the magazine success, but what was really needed was a school of landscape architecture. This letter was written in 1877, shortly before the magazine was actually printed. In other words, Professor Sargent, in Weidenmann's opinion, would have done better to start a landscape architecture school at Harvard where he taught.

Weidenmann can be considered the father of our present system for the educating of landscape architects. As early as his own college days, he crafted a college program, as well as allied apprenticeships, to best prepare for becoming a landscape architect. Throughout his career he advocated a similar program to others, and promoted the establishment of landscape architecture schools that would offer such a program. His performance as a landscape architect is a perfect example of one who could execute all aspects of planning from basic design to site engineering to architecture, as well as the horticultural aspects. There was no need for him to collaborate with experts in these fields in order to execute a plan.

It is unfortunate that Weidenmann did not live until 1900 because in that year Harvard President, Charles William Eliot, established both the Department of Landscape Architecture and the Department of Architecture through a gift from a generous donor. Mr. Nelson Robinson, of New York, had a son interested in architecture who died suddenly. Robinson approached President Eliot with an offer to establish an architecture program at Harvard as a memorial. Eliot told him that his son, Charles Eliot, a brilliant landscape architect who was associated with the Olmsted firm, had also recently died prematurely. Robinson was so moved that he expanded his offer to include the endowment of both Departments.

A year before, in 1899, a group of eleven landscape architects gathered in New York, and as a result of their meeting, the American Society of Landscape Architects was founded. This action, too, would have pleased Weidenmann as another means of standardizing the profession. Then in 1903, Professor Frank Waugh, a pomologist with great sensitivity for the natural landscape, founded a Department of Landscape Architecture at the University of Massachusetts, the first program at a Land Grant University. The movement was catching on, and progressively, throughout the twentieth century, schools of landscape architecture sprang forth throughout the country, and as graduates entered the profession, they joined the American Society of Landscape Architects. Today, one hundred years later, there are approximately sixty-five accredited schools of landscape architecture in the country, and the Society boasts about ten thousand members. In addition, forty-six of the fifty states have licensing laws, requiring that anyone practicing the profession must pass a standard examination. Weidenmann and his fellow practitioners of the nineteenth century would have hailed all of these important steps.

Weidenmann tombstone,
Cedar Hill Cemetery,
Hartford, Connecticut.

Afterword

Little is known about Jacob Weidenmann's wife and daughters, though it appears that the family was closely knit. The daughters revered their father, and he looked forward to spending much time with them. In the brief sketch that Marguerite wrote about her father, she said: "He was of a kindly, genial nature, trustful, and confident that everybody was as fair and honest in their dealings as he was himself."

He encouraged his daughters in the arts, particularly in drawing and painting. In November of 1882, Weidenmann submitted some of their paintings to The Art Students' League to see if his daughters might be accepted in one of the League's painting classes. Soon he received a letter in response saying that it was strongly recommended that they get more training in drawing before applying for painting instruction, and by so doing "will profit much more." The letter was signed by the eminent artist William Merritt Chase.

Evidently, Marguerite heeded Chase's advice because she became an accomplished artist and for many years was director of the French School of Fashion Illustrating and Commercial Art in New York, making her home at 762 Westminster Avenue. Following World War I, from 1918–1920, she served as a Reconstruction Aid in the Medical Corps of the United States Army.

Marguerite had a long and successful career in the art world; she lived eighty-seven years until 1955. When her last will and testament was probated the following year, it read that she left "the residue of my estate to the President and fellows of Harvard College, subject to the following restrictions:

> My beloved father, Jacob Weidenmann, having devoted his entire life to the practice of landscape architecture, with particular interest in designing and constructing of architectural structures, it is my wish and desire, in his memory, to encourage the said interests to which he was devoted. I, therefore, direct that the said bequest shall be used by the President and Fellows of Harvard College for the Department of Landscape Architecture, Graduate School of Design, and shall be known as "THE JACOB WEIDENMANN FUND."

She further stipulated that the income from the fund be awarded annually to a student who showed "outstanding ability and talent in designing of architectural structures relating to landscape architecture," and that the award be known as "THE JACOB WEIDEN-MANN PRIZE." It is fitting that the first Department of Landscape

Architecture to be established in the United States award a prize in Weidenmann's name since he had developed the model curriculum for educating landscape architecture students about ninety years earlier.

In that era before pensions and Social Security, when Jacob died, his family was left with little. While he received a settlement of about fourteen thousand dollars in the Mount Hope Cemetery case, much of this money was spent paying debts incurred during the two years prior to the case when he had had little employment. Then there were the hefty legal fees to pay, plus the cost of moving the family and their belongings back to New York. While the 1890s are often referred to as "The Gay Nineties," they were only gay for the wealthy. Economically, it was an unsettled decade, fraught with labor strikes, acute industrial unrest, and dissatisfaction with the McKinley tariff, to name just some of the causes of financial instability during these times. Money was tight and the economy was volatile; it was a difficult time for Weidenmann to try to reverse his financial downswing.

The week that Weidenmann died, his friend, architect George Keller, happened to be in New York. He received the news by telegraph from his home in Hartford, so he went immediately to the Weidenmann residence to see "poor Mrs. Weidenmann and her three helpless daughters." Mrs. Weidenmann told him that in recent years Jacob "had met with many reverses so that he has left but little or no living."

Keller wrote this news to Frederick Law Olmsted, and in his letter he asked if Olmsted's firm would be willing to carry on with Weidenmann's incomplete plans for Colonel Pope's park in Hartford, which, as we have noted previously, they did. He also inquired if Olmsted would meet with him in New York to go over all of Jacob's unfinished projects in order to give the Weidenmann family an idea of what work had been completed and the amount they should bill the clients. Because Jacob had run a one-man office, there was no one else to make these assessments.

Mrs. Weidenmann continued to live at 123 Berkeley Place in Brooklyn until her death, also of kidney failure, on December 22, 1909. Daughter Anna, who probably lived with her mother, died of heart failure on February 6, 1942, exactly forty-nine years to the day after her father's death. Elise died two years afterwards, and Marguerite survived until June 9, 1955. As mentioned previously, the entire family is buried at Cedar Hill Cemetery in Hartford.

Oil painting of Jacob Weidenmann, by his daughter Marguerite
Weidenmann, 1891, 18 x 15 inches.

Appendices

Residence and Office Locations of Jacob Weidenmann and his Family, 1856–1893

1857	50 Frankfurt Street, New York, NY; office, 21 Suffolk Street
1860–62	4 Sumner Street, Hartford, CT
1862–65	Trinity College, Hartford, CT
1865–1868	88 Church Street, Hartford, CT
1869	88 Church Street; office 13 Central Row, Hartford, CT
1871–72	No listing, Weidenmann in Switzerland
1872	55 College Street, Hartford, CT
1873	81 Buckingham Street, Hartford, CT
1875–77	203 East 57th Street, New York, NY; office, 11 Broadway
1878	203 East 57th Street, New York, NY; office, 953 Third Avenue
1879	114 East 103rd Street, New York, NY; office 11 Broadway
1880–85	114 East 103rd Street, New York, NY; office, 55 Bible House Office,
1886–88	22 East 25th Street, Chicago, IL
1889–93	123 Berkeley Place, Brooklyn, NY; office, 1 Third Avenue

Sources: City Directories for Brooklyn, NY, Hartford, CT, and New York, NY for the years indicated.

Projects in which Weidenmann was involved not listed in the text

James Breese Estate, Southampton, Long Island, NY
Chautauqua Point, Jamestown, NY
William Bayard Cutting Estate, Great River, Long Island, NY
Thomas Edison Property, Llewellyn Park, NJ
George Ehret Estate, location (?)
Fort Lee, Pierpont, NJ
Edward Hicks Estate, location (?)
Harrington Hotel, Demarest, Bergen County, NJ
The Johns Hopkins University Campus, Baltimore, MD
Memorial Park, Troy, NY
Henry Schulze Estate, Bellevue Street, Hartford, CT
Jacob Telfair Estate, Staten Island, NY
William Wadsworth Estate, Geneseo, NY
Edward Wicks Estate, location (?)

Sources: *A Sketch of the Life and Works of Jacob Weidenmann*, attributed to Marguerite Weidenmann (undated); *Hartford Courant*, September 8, 1863, for the Schulze Estate

Bibliography

Books

AE   Andre, Edouard. *L'Art des Jardins: Trait General de la Composition des Parcs et Jardins.* Paris: 1879.

AGRD   Andrews, Gregory, and David Ransom. *Structures and Styles.* Hartford, CT: 1988.

AJL   Alexopoulos, John. *The Nineteenth Century Parks of Hartford: A Legacy to the Nation.* Hartford: Hartford Architectural Conservancy, 1983.

BCCL   Birnbaum, Charles, and Lisa E. Crowden, eds. *Pioneers of American Landscape Design.* Washington, DC: United States Department of the Interior, 1993.

BE   Burke, Edmund. *A Philosophical Inquiry Into the Origin of Our Ideas of the Sublime and the Beautiful.* London: 1825.

BM   Bishop, Morris. *A History of Cornell.* Ithaca, NY: Cornell University Press, 1962.

BCH   Brown, Charles H. *William Cullen Bryant.* New York: Charles Scribner's Sons, 1971.

BLH   Bailey, Liberty Hyde. *The Standard Cyclopedia of American Horticulture.* VII. New York: Macmillan and Co., 1933.

CC   Cist, Charles. *Sketches and Statistics of Cincinnati in 1851.* Cincinnati, 1851.

CBR   *Commemorative Biographical Record of Hartford County, Connecticut.* Chicago: T.H. Beers and Co., 1901.

DA   *The Dictionary of Art,* Jane Turner, ed. New York: Grove, 1996.

DAB   *Dictionary of American Biography.* Dumas Malone, ed. New York: Charles's Scribner's Sons, 1934.

DSF   Delano, Sterling F. *Brook Farm: The Dark Side of Utopia.* Cambridge, MA: The Belknap Press of Harvard University Press, 2004.

DAJT   Downing, Andrew Jackson. *A Treatise on the Theory and Practice of Landscape Gardening Adapted to North America.* New York: G.P. Putnam and Co., 1849.

DAJR   Downing, Andrew Jackson. *Rural Essays,* George William Curtis, ed. New York: DeCapo Press, 1974.

DAPM   Dokart, Andrew S., and Mathew A. Postal. *New York City Landmarks, 3rd ed.* Hoboken, NJ: John Wiley and Sons, Inc., 2004.

EB   *Encyclopedia Britannica, Inc.* Chicago: William Benton, Publisher, 1966.

ECB   *Encyclopedia of Connecticut Biography.* Boston: American History Society, 1917.

EHP   Elston, Hattie P. *White Men Follow After,* 2nd ed. Spirit Lake, IA: Dickinson County Historical Society and Museum, 1990.

ERL   Edwards, Robert L. *of Singular Genius, of Singular Grace: A Biography of Horace Bushnell.* Cleveland, OH: The Pilgrim Press, 1992.

FMFD   Findlay, Mimi and Doris E. Friend. *The Lockwood-Mathews Mansion.* Norwalk, CT: The Lockwood-Mathews Mansion Museum, 1981.

FPH   Falk, Peter Hastings, ed. *Who Was Who in American Art, 1564–1975.* VI. Madison, CT: 1999.

FJPS   Favretti, Joy Putman. *Our Sacred Inheritance: An Historical Chronology of Hartford's Parks and Park System, 1815–1927.* Unpublished report, sponsored by The Knox Parks Foundation, Hartford, CT, 1976.

FRFJ   Favretti, Rudy J. and Joy Putman Favretti. *Landscapes and Gardens for Historic Buildings,* 2nd ed. Walnut Creek, CA: Altamira Press, 1991.

GLB   Goodheart, Lawrence B. *Mad Yankees.* Amherst, MA: University of Massachusetts Press, 2003.

HCL   Hartshorn, Cora L. *A Little History of Short Hills.* Short Hills, NJ: Millburn-Short Hills Historical Society, 1989.

HM   Hadfield, Miles, and Robert Harling and Leonie Highton. *British Gardeners: A Biographical Dictionary.* London: A Zwemmer, Ltd., and Conde Nast Publications, Ltd., 1980.

HW   Hubbell, Walter. *History of the Hubbell Family,* 1st ed. New York: 1881.

KJK   Kettlewell, James K. *Saratoga Springs: An Architectural History, 1790–1990.* Saratoga Springs, NY: Lyrical Ballads Bookstore, 1991.

LKYI   Larus, Kenneth, and Ira W. Yellen. *A Walk Around Walnut Hill in New Britain.* New Britain: 1975.

MBT   MacKay, Robert B., Baker, Anthony K. and Carol A. Traynor, eds. *Long Island Country Houses and Their Architects, 1860–1940.* New York: Society for the Preservation of Long Island Antiquities in Association with W.W.Norton and Company, 1997.

MC   Morison, Samuel Eliot, and Henry Steele Commager. *The Growth of the American Republic.* Vol. II. New York: Oxford University Press, 1954.

MDP   *Master List of Design Projects of the Olmsted Firm, 1857–1950.* Compiled by Charles C. Beveridge and Carolyn F. Hoffman. National Association of Olmsted Parks, 1987.

NNT   Newton, Norman T. *Design on the Land, The Development of Landscape Architecture.* Cambridge, MA: The Belknap Press of Harvard University Press, 1974.

NYCD   *New York, Brooklyn City Directories.*

OFKT   Olmsted, Frederick Law, Jr., and Theodora Kimball, eds. *Frederick Law Olmsted, Landscape Architect, 1822–1903.* Vol. I. New York: G.P. Putnam's Sons, 1922.

PALD   *Pioneers of American Landscape Design.* Charles A. Birnbaum, Robin Carson, eds. New York: McGraw Hill, 2000.

PKC   Parsons, Kermit Carlyle. *The Cornell Campus: A History of Its Planning and Development.* Ithaca, NY: Cornell University Press, 1968.

PW   Pierson, William H. *American Buildings and Their Architects.* New York: Anchor Books, 1980.

RDF   Ransom, David F. *Geo. Keller, Architect.* Hartford, CT: Hartford Architectural Conservancy in Cooperation with The Stowe-Day Foundation, 1978.

RJW   Reps, John W. *Views and View Makers of Urban America.* Columbia, MO: University of Missouri Press, 1984.

RLW   Roper, Laura Wood. *FLO: A Biography of Frederick Law Olmsted.* Baltimore, MD: The Johns Hopkins University Press, 1973.

SDTJ   Schuyler, David, and Jane Turner, eds. *The Papers of Frederick Law Olmsted. Vol. VI. The Years of Olmsted, Vaux, and Company, 1865–1874.* Baltimore: The Johns Hopkins University Press, 1992.

SSS   *Sticks, Shingles, and Stones. The History of Stewart Hartshorne's Ideal Community at Short Hills, New Jersey, 1878–1937.* Short Hills, NJ: 1980.

TJ   Turner, Jane, ed. *Dictionary of Art*, V. 18. New York: Macmillan Publications, 1996.

TP   Trowbridge, Peter, ed. *Public Space.* Cambridge, MA: Harvard University. 1975.

TW   *Twain's World: Essays on* Hartford's *Cultural Heritage. Hartford:* Hartford. Courant, 1999.

WBCH   Weidenmann, Jacob. *Beautifying Country Homes. A Handbook of Landscape Gardening.* New York: Orange Judd and Company, 1870.

WJMC   Weidenmann, Jacob. *Modern Cemeteries.* Chicago: The Monumental News Company, 1888.

WT   Whately, Thomas. *Observations on Modern Gardening.* London: 1877.

WD   Wiggins, David. *The Rise and Fall of the Allens.* Mount Horeb,
WI: Historical-Midwest Books, 2002.

ZJSR   Zukowsky, John and Ribbe Pierce Stimson. *Hudson River Villas.* New York: Rizzoli, 1985.

Journals, Newspapers, Pamphlets, Theses

AABN   *The American Architect and Building News. Vol.X, No. 299.*

AMFR   Alves, Mary M. and Rudy J. Favretti. *An Oasis on Main Street: The Landscape History of the Butler-McCook Homestead.* In the <u>Connecticut</u> <u>Antiquarian</u> Vol. XXXI, June 1984. Hartford, CT: Bulletin of the Antiquarian and Landmarks Society, Inc.

DAJ   Downing, Andrew Jackson, ed. *The Horticulturist.* Vol. IV, No. 1, July 1849. Albany, NY: Luther Tucker, publisher.

DL   *The Des Moines Leader.* Des Moines, IA.

DS   *Daily Saratogian.* Saratoga, NY.

DSM   *Official Souvenir, Dedication Soldiers' Monument, Central Park.* New Britain, CT: 1900.

HBB   Bushnell, Rev. Horace. *The Beginnings of Bushnell Park.* Hartford, CT: 1936. A reprint of an article first printed in <u>Hearth</u> <u>and</u> <u>Home</u>, Donald Mitchell, ed. 6 February 1869.

HC   *Hartford Courant.* Hartford, CT.

ISL   *The Iowa State Leader.* Des Moines, IA.

ISR   *The Iowa State Register.* Des Moines, IA.

LWB   Linden-Ward, Blanche. *The Greening of Cincinnati: Adolph Strauch's Legacy in Park Design.* In <u>Queen</u> <u>City</u> <u>Heritage.</u> V. 51, No. 1, Sept. Sept. 1993.

NT   Richardson, Ed, and Lee Monroe, *Notable Trees.* Hartford, CT: Institute of Living, 2001.

PT   *Persinger Times.* Des Moines, IA.

RCA   Rasmussen, Charles Allen. *State Fair: Culture and Agriculture in Iowa, 1854–1941.* PhD. Dissertation, Rutgers University, New Brunswick, NJ, 1992.

SDS   *Saratoga Daily Sentinel.* Saratoga, NY.

WAGA   *American Garden Architecture.* Part I, 1876–1877. Designed and executed by Jacob Weidenmann, landscape architect. New York.

Letters, Manuscript, Documents

ADW   Kroch Library, Cornell University, Ithaca, New York. The Andrew Dickson White Papers.

BA   A. Butckofer, Stadtarchivar, Winterthur, Switzerland, to Urs Hilfiker, Unterengstringen, Switzerland, July 13, 1995. Author's collection.

BMR   Mark Baeuer, Ranger, National Park Service, Hot Springs, AR, to Rudy J. Favretti, 7 March 2006.

CCP   Court of Common Pleas, Hartford County, Connecticut. Docket No. 1746, James Wells vs. Jacob Weidenmann, Feb. 1873.

CERT   Miriam and Ira D. Wallach Division of Art, Prints, and Photographs, The New York Public Library, Astor, Lenox and Tilden Foundations. *1876 Medal and Diploma for the Best System And Most Instructive Plans and Specifications for Practically Improving and Embellishing the Grounds, Survey, Drainage, Planting Plans, and general Map for improving "Masquetux" On Long Island. Awarded to Jacob Weidenmann, landscape Architect, by the Judges of Award of the International Exhibition in Philadelphia, 1876.*

CWL   Harriet Beecher Stowe Center, Hartford, Connecticut. William L. Collins Announcement of Plan for the City Park. May 20, 1861.

FM   Fatima Mahdi, Hastings Historical Society (NY), to Rudy J. Favretti, 14 March 2005.

FRJ   Favretti, Rudy J. *Cedar Hill Cemetery: An Historical Overview.* in Master Plan for Cedar Hill Cemetery, Halvorson Company, Boston, MA. 1996.

KT   Dr. Theodore Kaufman, interview by Rudy J. Favretti, Nov. 16, 2005.

LA   Linda Abrahms, Longmeadow, Massachusetts, to Rudy J. Favretti, November 26, 2005.

MD   Don Miles, Zimmer, Gunsul, Frasca Partnership, AIA, Des Moines, Iowa, to Bill McKegg, Iowa Capitol Complex Plan, Job No. 90473.01. 1999.

MPMO   Connecticut Historical Society Library, Hartford, Connecticut. Mary P. Morris Obituary Scrapbooks.

NYHS   New York Historical Society, Special Collections. New York, New York.

OP   The Library of Congress, Washington, DC. Papers of Frederick Law Olmsted.

PCR	I.A. Loffelmeir, Archivarntmann, Landeshauptstadt, Direktorium, Munich, Germany to Gunter Klein, Tenningen, Germany, August 8, 2000. Author's collection.
SHB	Collections of the Harriet Beecher Stowe Center, 77 Forest Street, Hartford, CT.
WEB	Wethersfield, Connecticut, Historical Society Library. Handwritten account of the Howe Estate. 1987.
WGE	Wait, Gary. *"The Tale of the Drawing Board"* (paper presented at meeting of the Weidenmann Society) Cedar Hill Cemetery, Hartford, CT, June 9, 2004.
WMS	Collection of the Hartford Parks Department, Hartford, CT. *A Sketch of the Life and Works of Jacob Weidenmann.* Attributed to Marguerite Weidenmann, Unpublished.
WT	American School for the Deaf, Hartford, Connecticut. Jacob Weidenmann to William W. Turner, Treasurer, [American Asylum for the Education of the Deaf and Dumb]. January 1, 1862.
WSC	Graduate School of Design Library, Harvard University. Schedule of Charges, Office of Jacob Weidenmann, c. 1884.
ZA	Dr. Alfredo Zavaletta, Upper Montclair, New Jersey, to Rudy J. Favretti, undated.

Maps and Plans

CMP	The Harriet Beecher Stowe Center Library, Hartford, CT "Plan of Cedar Mountain Cemetery, by Jacob Weidenmann, Landscape Gardener" (undated).
CR	Clark, Richard. "Map of Town of New Britain." Philadelphia: 1857.
HPE	Weidenmann, Jacob. " Plan of Hill Park Estate, Staten Island." (undated)
HRR	Harvey, Robert R. "Historical Grounds Report and Landscape Plan, Terrace Hill, State of Iowa Governor's Residence at Des Moines." 1985.
ICP	State Historical Society of Iowa Library, Des Moines. "Planting Map of the Iowa Capitol Grounds by Jacob Weidenmann, Landscape Architect." Drawing No. 962. (undated).
NBAS	Connecticut Historical Society, Hartford. " Map of Valuable Building Lots on Webster Street, Ellsworth Street, and New Britain Avenue, Hartford, Connecticut, Owned by C.L. Cleveland and William G. Allen. Drawn by Jacob Weidenmann." Hartford: Lithograph by E.B. Kellogg (undated).
PM	Records Office, City Hall, Des Moines, Iowa. "Plot Plan for Polk Hubbell Park." (undated)
WJGD	State Historical Society of Iowa Library, Des Moines. "Iowa State capitol Grounds, Grading and Drainage Map. Jacob Weidenmann, Landscape Architect. June 12, 1885."
WPCP	State Historical Society of Iowa, Des Moines. "Plan for the Center Pier," 6 Feb. 1891.
WPMS	State Historical Society of Iowa, Des Moines, Iowa. "Planting Map and Specifications," 15 December 1885.

Reports, Records

ARRI	Retreat for the Insane, Hartford, CT. Annual Reports of the Committee on Improvements. Nos. 37 (1861), 39 (1863).
BCCR	State Historical Society of Iowa, Des Moines. Board of Capitol Commissioners Report to His Excellency William Larrabee, Governor of the State of Iowa. Des Moines: January 3, 1890.
BPC	Annual Reports, City of Hartford, CT. 1859–1892.
CCC	Court of Common Council Records, City Hall, Hartford, CT.
CCO	City Clerk's Records, Hartford, CT.
CHR	Cedar Hill Cemetery, Hartford, CT. Reports for 1866, 1868, 1882, 1903.
DPH	Department of Public Health, Brooklyn, NY. Jacob Weidenmann's death certificate, issued to Rudy J. Favretti, February 2006.
HCR	Hartford, Connecticut City Reports.
REC	State Historical Society of Iowa, Des Moines. Report of the Executive Council to the 25th General Assembly, Des Moines: 1893–94.
RPC	Hartford Park Department Collection, Hartford, CT Report of the Park Committee.
WJCR	Koch Library, Cornell University, Ithaca, NY. Report for Improving and Laying Out the Cornell University Grounds. Jacob Weidenmann, Landscape Architect. June 8, 1870.

Websites

CB	*Columbia Bicycles-Columbia History.* Accessed 2 March 2006; available from www.columbiabikes.com/ditpages/10009.html
EB	*Eugene Achilles Baumann,* Accessed 19 February 2006; http://trees.ancestry.com
EH	Williamson, Samuel H. *Economic History Services.* Accessed 9 May 2006; available from: http://eh.net/hmet/. All dollar values in this text were on this site.
HCJ	*History, Jeffersonville, Indiana.* Accessed 27 January 2006; available from http://www.cityofjeff.net/history.html
LCT	Lyle, Charles T. *A Brief History of Boscobel.* Accessed 4 January 2006; Available from http://www.boscobel.org/history.html
SA	*Defense Supply Center, Philadelphia.* Accessed 21 January 2006; Available from http://www.dscp.dla.mil/history.htm
SP	Schmidt, Barbara. *Mark Twain and Karl Gerhardt.* Accessed 15 December 2005; available from http://www.twainquotes.com

Abbreviations:
C = Horace William Shaler Cleveland;
O = Frederick Law Olmsted, Sr.;
W = Jacob Weidenmann

Note:
Numbers following
bibliographic references
are page numbers.

Notes

Foreword

Pages   7   *Marguerite Weidenmann wrote:* WMS, 1. All biographical
                    material in the foreword is from this source.
        8   *One of the biggest:* WMS, 10-12.
            Yet in the "Master List of Design Projects": MDP.
        9   *Jacob Weidenmann is worthy:* OFKT, 130.

Chapter One—Formative Years

Pages   11 *A legend prevailed:* WMS, 2.
            By the early Nineteenth Century: BA.
            The Weidenmanns became: BA
            The younger Jacob Weidenmann: WMS, 3.
        12 *In 1847, Jacob and his brother:* WMS, 3; EB, 254.
            To enlarge his technical training: OP, W. to O. 22, Jan. 1885.
            Jacob Weidenman did well: WMS; DA, V. 18, 204-205.
            Many of these established artists: WMS, 4.
            While in Zurich in 1850: OP, W. to O., 22 July 1885.
        13 *The Weidenmann family's secure:* WMS, 6-8.
            Weidenmann subsequently heard: Ibid.
        14 *Shortly thereafter Weidenmann:* WMS, 8.
            We have no details: ZA.
        16 *Letters from home begged:* BA.
            On board the ship "Argonne": WMS, 10; BA.
            Jacob and Anna made their home: See appendix A.
        17 *When Weidenmann arrived:* BCH, 293; DAJR, 138.
        18 *In his Treatise, Downing:* DAJT, 31-37.
            Throughout this book: HM, 230.
            Simply defined: Ibid.
            The picturesque movement: HM, 171 and 230.
        19 *The picturesque was a major:* DAJT, 71.
            The writings of Downing and Loudon: WMS, 10.
            One contributor of essays: EB, DAJ.
        20 *The park's developer:* PWH, 422-431.
        21 *Jacob Weidenmann was acquainted:* DAB, V.4, 600.
        22 *One such commission was:* DAB, V.13, 32-33.
            The Minturn estate: FM
            One important commission: HPE.
        25 *Weidenmann's work in New York:* BA.

Pages   26   *Reverend Horace Bushnell:* CCO, "Petition of Samuel Tudor and
                   Others", #38.

                Bushnell was aware: ERL, 171–182; RPC, "Remarks by Horace
                   Bushnell," 5 Sept. 1853.

                Based on these principles: AJL, 15.

    27   *On September 5, 1853:* RPC, op.cit.

                According to a careful estimate: HBB.

                As acquisition of the last: CCO, 12 July 1858.

    28   *First prize was awarded:* PRC, 26 July 1858.

                There was dissatisfaction: AJL, 16.

                The new Park Board: BPC, First book of Reports, 1860.

                In one of her two written sketches: WMS, supplementary sketch; HC, 1
                   March 1878; CC.

    29   *Jacob Weidenmann had a Cincinnati:* LWB; BLH; PALD.

                By 1852, Adolph Strauch: OP, O. to William Robinson, March 1875.

                Weidenmann designed at least one major estate in Cincinnati: WBCH,
                   Plate VIII.

                Both gentlemen served on the newly formed Park Board: FJPS,
                   Appendix B, 99.

    30   *Many years later:* OP, J.C. Olmsted to Charles Eliot of Harvard,
                   8 April 1901.

                We do not know which of these stories: BPC, "First Book of Reports", 1860.

    32   *Jacob Weidenmann was eager to start:* See appendix A.

                Soon Weidenmann produced a new plan: WBCH, Plate IX.

                Access to the park: HBB.

                Weidenmann projected a stone terrace: CCO, Report #236, 28 Aug. 1865.

    34   *To further the two sections:* RDF, 129.

                Weidenmann drew his planting plan: WBCH, Plate IX.

                The Park Commissioners would be pleased: CWL.

                The grounds when first begun: WBCH, text to Plate IX; CCO,
                   Reports 237, 23. Nov. 1863, and 228, 12 Dec. 1863.

    35   *Two years later, in 1863:* FJPS, 21.

                Work progressed apace: RPC, Reports for1859–1892, 1.

                Obviously, Jacob Weidenmann: BA.

                It was not many years: CCC, 1870–1872 reports; RPC, "The Capitol
                   and Its Site", 5 Jan. 1872.

    36   *Cedar Hill Cemetery:* Cedar Hill is privately owned but serves
                   the public; hence its inclusion in this chapter.

                Rural cemeteries were burial grounds: DAJ, 9–12.

    37   *In 1863, a group of gentlemen:* CHR, 1903, 9.

                While the site selection committee: CHR, 23 June 1868

    38   *Now that Cedar Hill Cemetery:* IBID.

                The new rural cemetery site: CHR, 1882, 10.

                The site ascended gradually: CHR, 12.

    40   *This concept was actually:* WT, 2.

                An important part of the open lawn: WJMC, 5–10.

    42   *Jacob Weidenmann developed:* CHR, 1882, 11.

42   *Before Weidenmann began planning:* CHR, 1866, 32.
     None of Weidenmann's plans: CMP.

46   *While none of Jacob Weidenmann's:* WBCH, 29–31, 39–40.
     By the work season of 1865: CHR, 1866.

47   *On June 24, 1868:* HC, 23 June 1868.
     In the last quarter of the Nineteenth Century: FRJ.
     Jacob Weidenmann had proposed: WAGA, Plates 5, 6.

51   *At the south end of Hartford's:* CCC, 1811, 110; HCR, #3, 89.
     The new fence around: CCO, Feb. 1837; CCO, #58, #59, 6 Apr. 1852.
     Residents surrounding the Green: RPC, "Extract from Mayor Charles
             C. Chapman's Message, 1868."
     The triangular Green: WBCH, text for Plate V.

52   *Weidenmann's plan was:* CCO, #223, 9 March 1868, and #268,
             25 March 1869.
     Residents continued to apply pressure: HCR, 1871, 1; HCR, 18 April 1870, 29.
     There was much interest: HCR, 18 Apr. 1870, 29; TW, 74.

             Chapter Three — Hartford: Private Commissions

Pages   54   *In 1843, Dr. John Simpkins Butler:* MPMO, CBR.
             In Worcester, Butler: MPMO.
             The Retreat was founded in 1822: ARRI.
             Dr. Butler strongly believed: GLB.
             With this premise in mind: OP, Dr. Butler to), 6 June 1889; ARRI.

        55   *Large expanses of open lawn:* NT.

        56   *The plan that Olmsted and Vaux:* WBCH, text for Plate XXVII.
             The first step was to drain: ARRI, 1863.
             Retreat Park was officially: Ibid.

        58   *One recent August day:* WGE.

        59   *After a series of classes:* HC, 6 Nov. 1866.
             The landscape draftsman: RJW, 165.

        62   *In 1865, Miss Mary Sheldon:* AMRF. The entire passage on
                 the Butler Homestead is based on this reference except
                 as otherwise noted.
             John Butler, the son of Daniel: CBR.

        65   *Edmund Grant Howe was born:* ECB.
             The owner of the Brown Thomson: WEB.

        67   *James Leland Howard:* MPMO, V.LXI, 21 Apr. 1906.
             The Howards hired Jacob Weidenmann: WBCH, text for Plate IX.

        70   *Jacob Weidenmann's practice:* DSM; undated or documented
                 obituary in the collections of the New Britain Library,
                 Local History; ECB, 317.

        71   *Stanley owned a four acre site:* LKYI; WBCH, text for Plate VI.
             It is interesting to note: CR; OP, F. T. Stanley to O, 18 July 1867.

        74   *On Capitol Avenue:* Connecticut Historical Society, Hartford,
             photographic collection, 1926.
             Graperies were popular: WAGA, Plates 2, 3.

        75   *Jacob Weidenmann had:* NBAS.

Chapter Four—"Beautifying Country Homes"

<table>
<tr><td>Pages</td><td>76</td><td>Weidenmann's book, however: This entire chapter is based on an analysis of the book by the author (Favretti).</td></tr>
<tr><td></td><td>82</td><td>About the time that the book: BA.</td></tr>
</table>

Chapter Five—New York: Olmsted Alliance

<table>
<tr><td>Pages</td><td>84</td><td>Jacob Weidenmann spent: WMS
This was the last time: BA.
By November, 1871: OP, W. to O., 4 Nov. 1871.
On November 4, 1871: Ibid.</td></tr>
<tr><td></td><td>85</td><td>No doubt Weidenmann: MC, 67, 75, 113–114, 116, 250, 374.
More bad luck: HC, 20 July 1874; WMS.
He had previously: MPMO; CCP.
In the interim between his return: OP, O. to George E. Waring, 19 July 1874.
Weidenmann was then: SDTJ, 21.</td></tr>
<tr><td></td><td>86</td><td>Olmsted also offered him: WMS; OP, Cyrus Field to O., 26 Mar. 1878; DAB, V.6, 357–359.
Another commission that Weidenmann: OP, W. to O., 4 May 1872; W to O. 9 May 1872.
Mr. Greenleaf and his wife: LA.
Despite the unsettled decade: OFKT, 16.
Weidenmann continued executing: OP, Vaux to O., 28 Jan. 1873; W. to O., 28 Mar. 1873.</td></tr>
<tr><td></td><td>87</td><td>While Boscobel stands: LCT; ZJSR, 129.
Another significant project: OP, George Diven to W., 17 Jan. 1874; W. to O., 20 Jan. 1874; W. to O., 13 Feb. 1874.
By 1874 Olmsted and Weidenmann: See Appendix A.
On May 19, 1874: OP, O. to W., 19 May 1872.</td></tr>
<tr><td></td><td>88</td><td>Weidenmann took his time: OP, W. to O, 1 June 1874.
Even before Olmsted: OP, Draft of Announcement of Alliance, 1 May 1874.</td></tr>
<tr><td></td><td>89</td><td>As early as 1873: OP, Charles H. Dana to O., 20 Nov. 1873; Dana to O., 1 August 1874.
Dana planned to develop the tract: DSF, 313–314; DAB, V.5, 49.</td></tr>
<tr><td></td><td>90</td><td>Dana was a man who did: OP, Charles H. Dana to O., 27 Oct. 1874.
Thomas Wisedale was a young: RLW, 101, 377.
The project eventually came: MBT, 379.
Across the spine of Long Island: OP, H. B. Hyde to O., 12 Nov. 1874.</td></tr>
<tr><td></td><td>91</td><td>The generally rectangular: AE, 612–616.</td></tr>
<tr><td></td><td>94</td><td>The landscaping of "Masquetux": OP, W. to O., undated 1874: W. to O., 9 Nov. 1874; O. to Hyde, 13 Oct. 1874; O. to W., 9 Jan. 1875; Hyde to O., 11 Jan. 1875; Certificate on file at the New York Public Library, Print Collection, Miriam and Ira Wallach Division of Art, Astor, Lenox, and Tilden Foundation.</td></tr>
</table>

96   *Weidenmann also received:* AE, 612–616.

      Most of the "Masquetux" mansion: MBT, 418.

      Frederick Law Olmsted began: RLW, 373–378; OP, O. to W., 19 May 1874; W. (bill) to O., for summer work on Capitol Grounds in 1874.

98   *Quartermaster General Montgomery C. Meigs:* HCJ.

      In the spring of 1874: Op, Montgomery C. Meigs to O., 20 May 1874.

      Olmsted turned this project over: OP, W. to O., 2 May 1874.

      Weidenmann executed this project: OP, Meigs to O., 2 May 1874.

99   *Another government project initiated:* OP, O. to Stewart Van Vliet, 20 Sept. 1875; George K. Radford to O., 3 Aug. 1875, 21 Dec. 1875, 17 Jan. 1876; W. to O., 22 Dec. 1875; 21 Oct. 1875, 22 Oct. 1875, 7 Mar. 1876, 29 Nov. 1876; Quartermaster to O., 8 Jan. 1876, 17, Jan. 1876, 24 Apr. 1876; Quartermaster to W., 16 Dec. 1876; William E. Davis to O., 7 Jan. 1876.

      Jacob Weidenmann's business: WSC.

      This was a significant year: BMR.

100   *Between 1877 and 1878:* OP, O. to Robert R. Stevens, 25 may 1892; O. to Stevens, 7 Jan. 1893; O. to J.H. Willard, 4 June 1892.

      Saratoga Springs was named: Unidentified newspaper clipping dated 1 June 1882, in Local History Collections, Saratoga Public Library.

      In 1875, Frederick Law Olmsted: OP, O. to A.T. Perry, 17 April 1875.

101   *Weidenmann, well trained:* OP, W. to O., 20 Apr. 1875; DS, 7 June 1876.

      At the edge of the lower: WAGA, Plates 13–18. Unidentified newspaper article dated 1 June 1882, in Local History Collection, Saratoga Public Library.

      As landscape work in the Park: DS, undated; KJK, 173.

      Completed plans were presented: SDS, 13 July 1875.

104   *In the spring of 1874:* OP, W. to O., 2 May 1874; PKC, 20, 99.

      Obviously, President White: BM, 31–32.

      Weidenmann went to Ithaca: OP, W. to O., 2 May 1874; ADW, White to W., 9 Sept. 1874; BM, 148.

      After two days of making: ADW, White to W., 5 June 1874.

106   *Knowing that President White:* ADW, W. to White, 8 June 1874.

      Weidenmann's master plan: WJCR.

      His plan was soundly rejected: ADW, White to W., 8 Sept. 1874.

107   *Weidenmann worked together:* WMS; OP, W. to O., 10 Aug. 1874, 9 Aug. 1875, 14 Dec. 1875, 4 Aug. 1876; Calvert Vaux to O, no date 1872.

      During the 1870s: OP, Mrs. Lord to O., 9 May 1874, W. to O., 16 may 1874, W. to Mr. Lord (bill), 27 Mar. 1874.

      Another Olmsted reference: FMFD, 7–11.

      Lockwood died just seven: OP, Henry E. Pausch to O., 14 Aug. 1879.

      Weidenmann, on his own: WMS; DAB, V.11, 262.

110   *There were also several estates:* WMS; DAB, V.2, 373–374; KT.

      Up the river in Yonkers: WMS; DAB, V. 18, 537–544; ZJSR, 52.

      According to his daughter: WMS; HCL; SSS.

111   *Weidenmann had another New Jersey:* WMS; WAGA, Plate 1.

      Another project was the Villard Houses: WMS; DAPM.

Page 112 *Somehow Weidenmann heard:* BCCR, 7.

He started the project immediately: BCCR, 9, 10.

113 *The capitol building, begun:* ICP.

First, however, he addressed: Ibid.

Pedestrian walks lead: Ibid.

Weidenmann's design for the stair plaza: Ibid; on-site analysis
by the author.

The plaza, on axis with the Capitol's: Ibid.

114 *Weidenmann had three objectives:* WJGD, 12 June 1885.

Written comments accompanying: WJGD.

The Ground Committee, anxious: Ibid; ISL, 11 Sept. 1885; DL,
9 Nov. 1885.

116 *Weidenmann completed the planting plans:* WPMS.

The plant lists comprised: Ibid.

While many of these plants: Ibid.

Weidenmann was explicit: Ibid.

118 *It is clear in studying his "arrangements":* Ibid.

Concluding his twenty-eight page: Ibid.

Probably due to budget constraints: REC, 4.

119 *Weidenmann's work for the State Capitol:* OP, W. to O., 13 Mar. 1883:
ISR, 10 May 1880.

A mansion had already: WD, 1–3; HRR, Sect. II-C.

Benjamin Franklin Allen was considered: WD, 264–265; ISR, 10 May 1884.

The remaining forty-five acres: PT, 1 June 1884; HW, 226–227.

By mid-summer 1885: PT, 23 Aug. 1885; Weidenmann was always
careful to date his letters, but he often neglected to date his
plans. The plan for this residential park was not dated; however, "Tate's Atlas of Des Moines" dates the layout of the
project as 5 December 1885.

121 *While Weidenmann's plan:* PM.

123 *The Iowa State Agricultural Society:* RCA, 195.

The officers of the Agricultural Society: Ibid.

It is believed that Weidenmann: RCA, 196.

On September 3, 1886: ISR, 27 Aug. 1886.

124 *Beyond the racetrack:* Ibid.

Jacob Weidenmann also consulted: WMS; OP, W. to O., 6 Jun, 1886.

Research to date has not revealed: EHP.

Weidenmann's success with his various projects: OP, W. to O. 16 Jan. 1886.

125 *As he was contemplating:* OP, W. to O., 6 Jan. 86.

In considering the move: OP, W. to O., 22 Jan. 1885, 27 Jan. 1885.

Olmsted advised Weidenmann: OP, W. to O., 6 Jan. 1886.

Apparently, Cleveland and Olmsted: OP, C. to O., 25 July 1888.

In early May of 1886: OP, W. to O., 8 May 1886.

126 *Mr. William McCrea, president:* OP, W. to O., 30 July 1886.

Prior to Weidenmann's arrival: OP, C. to O., 6 Feb. 1888, 25 July 1888.

Cleveland tried to meet Weidenmann: OP, C. to O., 16 Feb. 1886.

Weidenmann worked on the plans: OP, W. to O., 30 July 1886.

Feeling a sense of total frustration: Ibid.

150   *Pope owned considerable real estate:* OP, W. to O., 6 Nov. 1892.

        Weidenmann completed the preliminary plans: Ibid.

        In January 1893: DPH.

        His body was held at Greenwood Cemetery: DPH.

        During Weidenmann's final illness: AGRD, 209.

151   *During the period when the Olmsteds:* RDF, 179–181.

        Another commission that ran concurrently: WMS.

        In the second half of the nineteenth: NNT, 307–317.

152   *The handful of qualified:* OP, C. to O., 24 Mar. 1886.

        In another letter Cleveland: Op, C. to O., 25 July 1883; RFJF, 40–41.

        Cleveland went on to say: OP, C. to O., 23 June 1889.

        Another point that troubled: RLW, 298.

        When I am employed: OP, Olmsted deposition of Feb, 1888 in the
            case of Weidenmann vs. Mount Hope Cemetery.

        Another landscape architect: GF, 5 Sept. 1888, 355.

153   *They all complained about:* OP, W. to O., 15 Sept. 1887.

        Weidenmann asserted that: RLW, 394, 403; OP, W. to O., 18 Nov. 1884.

        He also was an ardent: RLW, 394; OP, W. to O., 18 Nov. 1884.

154   *The curriculum that Weidenmann:* OP, W. to O., 14 Dec. 1887.

        Weidenmann actually took: OP, W. to O., 30 April 1875; NYHS, Misc.
        Mss. Weidenmann Jacob, F.W. Bonn to Weidenmann, 27 Sept. 1882.

        While taking on apprentices: RLW, 405.

155   *It is unfortunate:* NNT, 336.

        A year before, in 1899: NNT, 385.

157   *Little is known about Jacob:* WMS.

        He encouraged his daughters: NYHS, Misc. <ss., William Merritt
        Chase, W. to William Merritt Chase, 21 Nov. 1882; NYCD, 1915–1916;
        NYHS, Misc. MSS Weidenmann Jacob, Official letters relative to
            her Marguerite Weidenmann's service as a Reconstruction
            Aide, U.S. Army, 1918–20.

        My beloved father: Bequest in the will of Marguerite Weidenmann,
            8 May 1956, filed in the Archives of Harvard University,
            Pusey Library.

158   *The week that Weidenmann:* SHB, George Keller to O., 14 Feb. 1893.

        Keller wrote this news: Ibid.

        Mrs. Weidenmann continued: Cedar Hill Cemetery Death and Burial
            Records, #2297.

Acknowledgements

Writing a book is quite like building a garden wall; there are many parts that must fit together securely, and the whole must be stabilized by substantial cornerstones.

In writing this book, there have been two major cornerstones. The first is my wife, Joy, who initially discovered the importance of Jacob Weidenmann's influence through her research on the evolution of the Hartford, Connecticut, park system for the Knox Parks Foundation. That was well over thirty years ago.

It was she who first suggested that I conduct further research on Weidenmann, and then write an account of his career. Through the years she has lovingly encouraged me, and she assisted with the research when her schedule permitted. Without her encouragement and support, I would never have succeeded.

The other solid cornerstone is F. Aldrich Edwards, who for several years was Executive Director of Cedar Hill Cemetery. It was his idea to create the Cedar Hill Cemetery Foundation to accomplish worthy projects related to Cedar Hill. Aldy suggested that the first project of the Foundation should be to fund my remaining research in order to publish the results in a book. The Foundation's directors unanimously accepted the idea. Since completion of the manuscript, he has led the effort to raise publication funds. Because of his diligence you hold this book in your hands.

In 1977 I began consulting at "Monticello," the home of Thomas Jefferson. William Beiswanger, the architectural historian there, to whom I was responsible, was one of the few people I had ever met who knew of Jacob Weidenmann, and over the years, he has nudged me along. In fact, he sold me my copy of Weidenmann's *Beautifying Country Homes*; I had been seeking one for many years.

In a similar manner, Robert L. Newall, Jr., my friend and colleague on the Cedar Hill Cemetery Board, took a keen interest in my research from the start, and continued to be a staunch supporter until his death in 2006.

Reading the Olmsted Papers for the nineteen years of the Olmsted-Weidenmann alliance was a long and arduous task. The friendly cooperation of the staff at the Library of Congress, who so willingly sent microfilm reels to the Babbidge Library at the University of Connecticut for me to read, was heartening. This relay of reels was efficiently orchestrated by Lynn Sweet and Lana Babij at the Library. Also, Michael Young, the Art and Design Librarian, helped me to research many art issues related to Weidenmann's career. Suzanne Staubach, of the UConn Co-op, gave valuable advice throughout the project, both for writing and publishing.

Specialists at other university libraries gave generously of their time. At Cornell's Kroch Library, Nancy Dean and staff provided me letters and documents related to Weidenmann's master plan for the campus. I am also indebted to Mary Daniels, head of Special Collections at the Graduate School of Design at Harvard, who made available a complete first issue of Weidenmann's *American Garden Architecture*. Dean Alan Altschuler, and Professor Niall G. Kirkwood, head of the Department of Landscape Architecture, Graduate School of Design, were kind to give permission for me to review the papers related to Marguerite Weidenmann's bequest for the creation of the Weidenmann Prize. Barbara Meloni dug deeply into the Pusey Archives to find these papers. The staff at Columbia University's Avery Library also searched their collections for me.

At the New York Public Library, where the largest collection of Weidenmann material is held, Thomas Lisanti and Margaret Glover were most patient advisors, and they allowed me to spend days studying this important collection. They then granted permission to reproduce selections for this book.

Several blocks uptown at the New York Historical Society, the library staff in Special Collections could not have been more helpful in making their collection of Weidenmann letters, as well as his gold nugget, available. Jill Reichenbach successfully searched for the Weidenmann portrait that was filed in the depths of their storage facilities.

The Library Staff at the Staten Island Institute of Arts and Sciences graciously answered my many questions and assisted with my searches for the better part of a day. The Hill Park Estate plan was copied for me to study and use in this book.

Several state and local historical societies and organizations in Connecticut were generous with their time and materials. At the Connecticut Historical Society, Judith Ellen Johnson and Nancy Finlay spent hours leading me to pertinent source material. Wilson Faude also led me to some important documents and maps in that collection. At the Wethersfield Historical Society, Elaine St. Onge came to the rescue concerning the Howe Estate. Beverly Lucas, of the Connecticut Antiquarian and Landmarks Society shared their rare Weidenmann plan and documents for the Butler Homestead, and Beth Giard did the same for the Keller letters and the Cedar Mountain Cemetery plan in her custody at the Harriet Beecher Stowe Center in Hartford.

Many individuals assisted me with various aspects of Weidenmann's commissions in the Hartford area. They are: Linda C. Abrams (of Longmeadow, MA), Dr. Bruce Clouette, Jared Edwards, Edward Richardson, and Gary E. Wait. David Ransom always inquired about my research and offered insight. Superior Court Judge Patricia Swords helped me unravel some of the legal issues in which Weidenmann was involved in Hartford. Patricia Watson, librarian for Local History at the New Britain Public Library, responded to my many queries by phone, and she also gave access to information on Timothy Stanley at the library.

In New York State, Fatima Mahdi, of the Hastings Historical Society, promptly answered my e-mails and phone calls regarding "Locust Grove." Field Horne, in Saratoga Springs, directed me to various repositories and documents on Congress Park, and he also shared some of his research with me. The library staff in the Saratoga Springs Public Library, Local History Division, gave generously of their time, as did the staff at the Historical Society of Saratoga Springs.

Several of our personal friends assisted, too. Urs and Isabel Hilfiker hosted us in Switzerland when we went there to study Weidenmann's early years. They also obtained for me the recorded vital statistics about his family. Armgard and Gunter Klein gathered information from the Akademie der Bildenden Kunste, as well as from the police registry in Munich, Germany, for the years that Weidenmann spent at school in Munich (during those revolutionary times, outsiders had to register with the police). The late Dr. Alfredo Zavaletta, a native of Peru, helped me to research the Hacienda "La Molina" in Lima. Dr. Ted Kaufman checked some details on Weidenmann's work on Bliss Park in Brooklyn, as did Robert MacKay for "Masquetux."

There was very little information concerning Weidenmann's work in Iowa, so I had to rely on the good auspices of many individuals there. At the State Historical Society of Iowa, in Des Moines, and at Tower Hill, the staffs could not have been more cooperative. Jeffrey C. Dawson, Sharon Avery, Bennett Berry, Kristen Langstraat, Brian Browning, and David Cordes helped in every way to make my week-long visit there productive. Rosa Snyder was most generous in sharing her research on the State Capitol. John Zeller presented me with copies of his personal indexes of the nineteenth century Des Moines newspapers that pertained to Weidenmann's work, greatly expediting my research. Ruth Lukes and Cindy Shubert provided me with a good history of Spirit Lake.

I was fortunate to have excellent technical guidance as well. I am grateful to my editor, Elizabeth M. Lockyer, who was very patient and offered many suggestions for improvement. I also thank Nathan Garland who not only designed the book, but as a friend, offered other helpful hints. Michael Wengloski, of the Photo Connection in Colchester, CT, dealt patiently with my photographic requests. I will always be grateful to our son, Giovanni Favretti, whose critical reviews of the manuscript helped to make it more interesting.

Financial support of the donors to the Cedar Hill Cemetery Foundation enabled the completion of research and the publication of this book. Gifts and grants were received from the Aetna Foundation, Architectural Heritage Foundation, James W. Batten and John V. Shepard, Sally E. Newell Belding, Cedar Hill Cemetery Association, Margaret M. Cunningham, Clare and Jared Edwards, F. Aldrich Edwards, Gordon and Molly Fowler, IBM Corporation, Mary Jeanne Jones, Russell and Barb Jones, David and Kay Long, Susan S. Menson, Robert L. Newell, Jr., The Saunders Foundation, and Virginia Way. Their support enhances this remembrance of Jacob Weidenmann's life and work and is gratefully appreciated.

Having worked on this book for almost forty years, it is inevitable that I may have missed an individual or two who also assisted. If I have, I apologize, and can only say that it was not intentional. I am grateful for everyone's assistance whether he/she is listed or not. This has been a long but enjoyable road, and part of the fun was working with all who generously assisted. Thank you all.

Rudy J. Favretti
P.O. Box 403
Storrs, CT 06268

Index

"Professor Favretti has made an important contribution to the history of landscape architecture in this country. He has given substance and significance to Jacob Weidenmann—one of the small group that Frederick Law Olmsted considered prime practitioners of his art, and the person who was his valued collaborator during a full decade of practice."

> Charles E. Beveridge, Series Editor,
> *The Papers of Frederick Law Olmsted*

"Rudy Favretti evocatively illuminates the career of an elusive pivotal designer and educator that made significant contributions to the development of the profession of landscape architecture in America. In the process, Favretti secures Weidenmann the attention and respect that has been previously afforded to Olmsted, Cleveland, and Vaux."

> Charles A. Birnbaum, FASLA, FAAR,
> Founder and President,
> The Cultural Landscape Foundation, and Series Editor,
> *Pioneers of American Landscape Design*

"Following four decades of research, Rudy Favretti has written a fascinating account of Jacob Weidenmann, one of America's premier nineteenth-century landscape architects. This comprehensive and engaging work clearly documents the many contributions Weidenmann made to the profession of landscape architecture as we know it today."

> James R. Cothran, Fellow,
> American Society of Landscape Architects

"Favretti has created a balanced and compelling portrait of the landscape architect Jacob Weidenmann. Written with clarity and intelligence, his deeply informed and lavishly illustrated volume is utterly fascinating. This wonderfully textured portrait of Weidenmann is a book that every student of landscape architecture needs to read. An absolute gem."

> Wendell Garrett,
> Sotheby's consultant on American decorative arts
> and Editor-at-Large of *The Magazine Antiques*

"In this richly illustrated biography, Favretti—the dean of American landscape history—rescues Weidenmann from the shadows of history and elevates him to his rightful place alongside Olmsted as one of America's foremost landscape designers."

> Scott Kunst, Old House Gardens—Heirloom Bulbs,
> Ann Arbor, Michigan

The author

Rudy J. Favretti is a Connecticut native, born in Stonington and educated in the public schools there. He holds degrees in horticulture, landscape architecture, and regional planning from the University of Connecticut, the University of Massachusetts, and Cornell.

In 1955, he joined the faculty of the University of Connecticut where he served for 33 years as professor of landscape architecture, during which time he founded the nationally accredited landscape architecture program.

He also conducted a private practice specializing in landscape preservation. A few of his over 500 commissions include plans for Thomas Jefferson's "Monticello," George Washington's "Mount Vernon," James Buchanan's "Wheatlands," James Madison's "Montpelier," Strawbery Banke in Portsmouth, New Hampshire, the Emily Dickinson House in Amherst, Massachusetts, Bartram's Garden in Philadelphia, and Bok Tower Gardens in Lake Wales, Florida. He is also the author of numerous journal articles, and eleven other books.

Other books by Rudy J. Favretti

Growing for Showing (1961)

Colonial Gardens (1971)

Once Upon Quoketaug (1974)

Highlights of Connecticut Agriculture (1976)

Trails for the Future (1976)

For Every House a Garden,
with Joy P. Favretti (1977)

Landscapes and Gardens for Historic Buildings,
with Joy P. Favretti (1978)

Landscapes and Gardens of Virginia,
photography by Richard Cheek (1993)

Jumping the Puddle (2002)

*Mansfield Four Corners: What it Used to be
and George Washington Didn't See* (2003)

Il Salto del Fosso (2004)

Jacob Weidenmann
pioneer landscape architect

was printed in four-color process and duotone
on archival paper in Italy by Amilcare Pizzi.
This first edition of three thousand books
were all hardbound.

It was set in a contemporary version of Caslon.
This classic English typeface was based
on Dutch models and produced by William
Caslon (1692–1766). Its ongoing use in
the United States began in the colonial era.

The book was designed by Nathan Garland
in New Haven, Connecticut.